Sharon Beekmann's personal story provides a needed message of both alarm and hope. Her shout of warning says that seeking spiritual experience apart from the absolutes of God's Word is a sure road to deceived bondage. Her message of hope assures that the darkest spiritual bondage can be broken when Christ is embraced, and darkness is renounced.

—*Dr. Mark I. Bubeck,*
*International Center for Biblical Counseling*

Numerous people in the West are searching for meaningful spiritual experience by contacting "angels" and "spirit guides." Sharon Beekmann's story tragically illustrates that not all spirits have our best interest in mind. The good news is that the Lord Jesus Christ offers deliverance and freedom from their deceit and tyranny.

—*Dr. Clinton E. Arnold, Professor of New Testament,*
*Talbot School of Theology*

Sharon Beekmann is a committed Christian who attends our church faithfully and serves Christ well. Sharon has unusual discernment with regard to the spiritual pitfalls of a fallen world. I believe that through this book, the light of Christ will shine on many.

—*Dr. James S. Dixon Senior Pastor 1982-2013,*
*Cherry Hills Community Church,*
*Highlands Ranch, Colorado*

# RESCUED AND REDEEMED

*How to Discern Demons from the Divine*

*by*

## Sharon T. Beekmann

# RESCUED AND REDEEMED

Copyright © 2018 by Sharon T. Beekmann

Previously Published as
*Enticed by the Light:*
*The Terrifying Story of One Woman's Encounter with the New Age*

Christian Discernment Resources

Packaged and published by
Illumify Media Global
www.IllumifyMedia.com
Write. Market. Publish. SELL!

Print: 978-1-949021-05-9
eBook: 978-1-949021-06-6

*To those who are on a spiritual quest to know God…*

# CONTENTS

# Preface

TEN YEARS AFTER MY CONVERSION in 1987, Zondervan published *Enticed by the Light: The Terrifying Story of One Woman's Encounter with the New Age*. It was a bold unmasking of demonic deception and influence, and of Jesus Christ's absolute authority and power over the demonic realm. The book exposed demonic deceit; it riveted, astounded, and sometimes frightened readers. Readers asked many questions about what demons could and could not do, given the gospel of Jesus Christ. They expressed concern for friends and family who dabbled in occult practices. Some told stories of ghosts and menacing spirits appearing in the night. Some asked for help to distinguish between mental illness and demonization. A few described similar experiences. Most lacked the biblical knowledge to help them understand how my story might apply to them.

Ten years after its publication, I received a MDiv, and the following summer, I was ordained as Teaching Elder in the Evangelical Presbyterian Church. In 2012 I co-authored *Silencing Satan: Biblical Handbook in Biblical Demonology* with Rev. Dr. Peter G. Bolt.

I begin my book series, "Christian Discernment Resources," with a revised edition of my testimony. It has a new title, *Rescued and Redeemed: How to Discern Demons from the Divine*, and revised content. I added chapter introductions and stories that vividly depict God's authority over the demonic realm.

My motivation for writing the series evolved as I observed that Christians in general were ill-equipped to discern the spirits and underestimated the power of the gospel. Some were even offended at the suggestion that they should consider the source of spiritual inspirations, visitations from the dead, practices such as yoga and Hindu meditation, and insights obtained in altered states of consciousness. Why is this so? Though not exhaustive, I offer the following.

First, Christians are more inclined to seek counsel from mental-health practitioners and experts in related fields than the guidance and instruction from God and his Word. God's involvement in daily life, miracles, and other supernatural encounters are treated as stand-alone stories—fascinating but irrelevant in daily living. Lacking biblical knowledge, the conventional wisdom is that Satan and the demons cannot influence a life unless invited in. Perhaps God, too, stands in the wings waiting for someone to need him.

Second, not that long ago, the Bible had authority as God's revelation of himself and the supernatural realm. That is not true in many churches today. Christians tend to rely on personal experience, stories of friends, the Internet, and popular culture to assess the source of, say, visions, intuitions, and spirit manifestations. If the vision and experience look and feel good, the source is God. If it's dark and menacing, the source is evil, perhaps Satan. Most neither see the need to further test the source of it nor do they know how.

Third, social media, and the entertainment and health industries have stepped into the gap with a plethora of stories and teachings on the supernatural realm. Films saturate our culture with tales of magicians and sorceresses, warring gods, and spirits of the dead conversing with the living. They elevate people with the "gift" to foretell future events and look to them for information on the spiritual realm. Health and wellness magazines promote yoga and meditation practices that are based on Hinduism to achieve peace and "well-balanced" bodies. The result is that people develop their doctrine of angels, demons, and the spiritual realm from popular culture.

Fourth, the ordinariness of evil obscures its lethality. I once stared at the swept-clean, small barracks and ovens at Dachau. They looked so ordinary. Absent survivors' stories, no one could know the scale of evil done there. Even the efficiency and mechanization of the death camps enabled workers to perform ghastly tasks without the burden of guilt. Evil is like that. In its most devious manifestations, evil infiltrates cultures in ordinary ways so that it passes as something good. One doesn't think to call on the Savior or to examine Scripture to see if this is of God. But the banal façade of evil cannot last. Like a voracious parasite, it cannot stop itself from destroying its host.

Fifth, church leaders and pastors are reluctant to focus on the demonic realm, and when they do, they use broad-brush references to a spiritual war in the heavens. Many seminaries and pastors sincerely believe that it is wrong to give Satan and the demons attention, and furthermore, it is unnecessary given Jesus' defeat of them. They preach that as Christians address sin and love and obey Jesus, they nullify demonic involvement. Lastly, focusing on the devil scares people and might divert interest in the gospel. Of course, this begs the question—what if it's true? What if it's true that we have a spiritual enemy that schemes and works to destroy people, even Christians?

These observations suggest that a humanistic and postmodern worldview that dominates popular culture has infiltrated the church. To counter its influence, mature Christians must learn to discern good and evil (Heb. 5:14). They do so by remaining close to the Savior and studying his Word. Only then can Christians assess if something is from God or a demon. Without the Savior and his Word, we are lost indeed.

*Rescued and Redeemed: How to Discern Demons from the Divine* begins with demons possessing me and ends with God securing me through faith in Jesus Christ. People frequently ask whether Satan continues to attack me. I reply, "Yes, he harasses me, but no more than he does other Christians. I am simply aware of his tactics. Such knowledge does not frighten me, because of the power and authority of Jesus to rescue and redeem lives—our minds, hearts, bodies, and relationships."

In daily life, I focus hard on Jesus Christ and keep Satan's activity in my peripheral vision. While aware of his devices, I give him no more attention than he deserves. I live an ordinary—albeit radical—Christian life of obedience and dependence on God and his Word. In tough times, I am God's foot soldier. By his grace, I willfully remain strong in the Lord and persevere in faith.

God has redeemed every aspect of my life. He sends me out, as he does all Christians, to make disciples. To God be the glory,

—*Sharon Beekmann*

# Acknowledgements

To PROTECT THEIR PRIVACY, I have given fictitious names to some of the people I write about in this book. The exceptions are members of my family, Jane Roberts, Johanna Michaelsen, Dr. Mary Claire (Tad) Frantz, Pastor Erwin Prange, Reverend David Stark, Dolores Howe, Virginia Satir, Rebecca and Ron Faillaci, Dr. Gordon Lewis, and Dr. Neil Anderson.

Many people have walked alongside and loved me as I have matured in my relationship with God. I thank my family and people at Corona Presbyterian Church, Christ Episcopal Church, and Cherry Hills Community Church for their prayers, love, and steadfastness and for sharing the Word of God with me.

# PROLOGUE

# They Took Me Captive

### January 1985

I SAT FORWARD ON THE couch to plant my feet on the floor and then wrapped my arms around my ribs, hesitated, and with a nod, whispered, "Yes, this is right for me." Resolved, I closed my eyes, breathed deeply, and entered the silence where I believed the physical and spiritual meet. Years earlier, when first learning to meditate at a spiritualist church, I had struggled for an hour to blot out the room and quell thoughts rummaging in my mind, but tonight I quieted instantly. I waited for my guides to appear.

I concentrated on the dark blank screen in my mind's eye, and soon the back of King Egglog's head materialized. A gold crown embedded with rubies and sapphires sat squarely on his mangy red hair, and he exuded vibrations of warmth, strength, trustworthiness, and wisdom—reflections of his character that endeared him to me and prompted me to seek his counsel the past seven years. He probably suspected the intent of my call, and yet he respectfully waited for me to say it. As the leader of my spirit band, coordinator of the five spirits I channeled, it was proper that he be the first to know.

He turned until his profile filled my vision and then he spoke telepathically, "You have something you want to tell us?"

"Yes. I've decided to stop channeling. You have been so very kind and helpful to me and others, but it's time for me to move on. I want to explore other aspects of my life now, so I must say good-bye."

"We're sorry to hear this, but of course you must do what you think best, and we will respect your decision. We thank you for giving of your time and energy, and we wish you the best. The others will say good-bye now." And they did, one by one. The last to come was Seth.

He whimpered, "I'm so disappointed, and I don't know what I'm going to do. What if we can't find a replacement . . . what will we do? Please don't ask us to leave . . . please?"

"Oh, you'll be able to find someone else, and like I said, I must move on with my life."

"It doesn't seem fair. You could have given us some warning."

"I've been thinking of it for a while, but I wanted to be sure before announcing it to you."

Angry, he said, "All right, if you must!" He left abruptly without saying good-bye.

"That's strange," I thought, "I've never known Seth to behave like that. Guess spirits have feelings too. He'll be okay once he gets used to the idea."

Staring at the dark in my mind, I breathed a sigh, dropped my shoulders, and opened my eyes. It was over, finished.

I fingered the rust-colored strings woven through a pillow the color of sand beside me then leaned back against others like it lining the couch. Behind me were the floor to ceiling windows that ran along the front of my house, and straight ahead in the dining area an overhead light reflected off the glass covering my dining room table. Outside a horn honked and a dog barked. Then silence returned to my home in the Denver suburbs.

"It's time to move on," I sighed, "one phase over and another beginning." Of course, I had my reasons to stop channeling. Somewhere in the quest to explore my spirituality, I lost the vibrancy of self-confidence that once characterized my personality. I felt fragile, and a coldness advanced from the inside out. I had other concerns.

My guides asked to communicate with me often when I was not attending the spiritual development class. Their requests disrupted my life, making it difficult to concentrate, attend to my business, and converse with people. Then last month they had asked me to predict a nuclear holocaust. The message frightened me, and I knew it would frighten others. Heretofore their readings had been positive, uplifting, and never terrifying, and I wanted no part of this prophecy, true or not.

I leaned forward and thought, "I'm free to get on with my life now." I was concluding a journey that stretched back to 1977, and through the years I had devoured books and participated in various adventures in consciousness and spiritual expression. In 1982, at the peak of my fascination with the spiritual realm, my marriage unexpectedly dissolved, and now I could see that during those years I had let go of many people. I needed to get back into the mainstream of life. I looked forward to spending time with my nine-year old son, Michael, further developing my psychotherapy practice, completing my doctorate, widening my circle of friends and using my mind for my own thinking again.

My life was my own—wasn't it? No spirit could influence me without my consent, at least that's what I believed. My spirit guides were required, by some law of nature, to respect my right to conduct my life as I saw fit. When giving a reading or teaching,

I allowed them to communicate through me. It was inconceivable to me that spirits had the ability and right to usurp a life—take it over as if their own. What kind of world would this be if that were allowed? What manner of existence would human beings have if spirits could do that? It defied everything I believed about the way the universe worked. Michael was at his father's house for the weekend, and so tonight I did his chores and mine, turned off lights, let the dog out, and locked doors before climbing the stairs of my trilevel home and going to bed. I fell asleep thinking, "When the universe closes one door, it opens another. Where will my path lead this time?"

The next morning was Saturday, errand day, and before rising, I snuggled under my down-filled comforter and whispered, "Yes, it's right." But the words were barely uttered when a foreboding permeated every pore and Seth whispered in low, menacing tones, "Couldn't leave, Sharon. Sorry. Have to stay. Nowhere to go. Sorry."

I stilled myself, "No. . . . No. . . . Can't be," I thought. Then I said aloud, "Seth, leave. You've got to leave. You'll find something."

"No. You . . . " and he flung a string of crude names at me. I reeled, recovered, and vied for my mind, but he muscled me out. My insides trembled, and the horror dawned that overnight my wise, caring counselor had shed his skin, and a sadistic tormentor occupied my mind and body.

# CHAPTER 1

# I Lost Control of My Life

*He was a murderer from the beginning, not holding to the truth, for there is no truth in him. When he lies, he speaks his native language, for he is a liar and the father of lies* (John 8:44b).

*I was ignorant of the way God's universe worked and had no defense against my spiritual adversary. I knew nothing of his strategy, capability, or power. I didn't know that God existed and watched over me.*

I LEAPED FROM BED, DRESSED amid his vile cursing, ran downstairs, and paced the house. Aloud I cried to my guides, "Help me! What happened? Help me!" But I only heard, "You're mine to do with as I please."

Clenching my head with my hands, I stopped to stare at the slate-gray ashes in the fireplace, whirled, and ran out the front door and down the street. My heart raced. I sweated. Yes, I lived, but I dared not stop, lest their incessant cursing demolish me. After a couple blocks, I slowed my pace, grabbed my sides, and screamed, pleaded, "Leave me. Let me be!" They mocked and mimicked me. That was my defining moment: my former life was over. Spirits, more evil than I imagined existed, had invaded me, and nothing I did loosened their grip on my life. What I believed and who I was meant nothing to them, and in that sense, their utter contempt and torture of me wasn't personal. I ran until my sides ached and my lungs could take no more.

That afternoon, to divert my attention, I went to a movie entitled *A Passage to India*. An uncanny choice, the story was about an English woman who was driven to discover something she could not define and lost herself along the way. While in India, she made a daylong trek to some caves known to have mysterious, spiritual energies that could produce disastrous effects on people.

I scarcely breathed as she entered the cave. The woman lit a match and lifted it so that its flickering cast light on her face. Intense emotions overtook her, and her eyes rolled back. The screen blackened. "Her enemy is spiritual," I whispered. "What has happened to us? Where do these spirits come from, and what right do they have to take over a life? What sort of universe do we live in?" I clung to the arms of my seat as the woman bolted from the cave. Thorns bloodied her legs, arms, and face as she fled. A drug-induced coma quieted her mind. What would quiet mine?

As I left the theater, I fixed my eyes on a thin black line in the red carpet and followed it through the lobby. Bizarre thoughts and feelings erupted in me, but unlike her, I knew the source of them. I claimed none of them as mine. "These spirits surely will see how meaningless this is. They will come to their senses and let me go."

I couldn't know that no deep thoughts motivated them. No inherent goodness confused, confounded, or distracted them. There was no goodness in them. None! For the first seven months, I pleaded for my life in an attempt to appeal to some sense of fair play, some moral fiber in them. There was none. No goodness, no moral compass, and no heart dissuaded them. They toyed with me like a cat with a half-dead mouse. Such evil contradicted everything I believed about the way the world worked. They never explained or justified themselves. I faced the full extent of evil incrementally. I simply couldn't take it in all at once.

I struggled to complete simple tasks. While grocery shopping, I stuffed my list in my pocket and headed for the aisle containing soups. Spirits ranted in my mind. As I stood in front of the rows of cans and stacked envelopes, my mind froze. What did I want?

A spirit answered my thought, "Sharon, I know best what you want. And I must teach you this . . . your mind belongs to me now. I like tomato soup, and so do you. Remember? Bright girl like you can't remember what you like?"

Silence. The cans lined up like soldiers, each one resembled the other, and not one held my attention, "Was it tomato?"

He answered, "Oh, we can never have enough tomato soup, let's buy it."

Suddenly I longed for tomato soup and then developed an insatiable craving for it.

"See what I can do! Now let me show you how I can make you hate it." And he did. "Chicken soup. Was it chicken soup you wanted?"

I spied the chicken soup among the cans, and though I could not be sure the prompting to buy it came from me, the thought somewhat resonated. I whispered, "Chicken soup, yes, that was it." Through the spirit's objections, I retrieved my list and saw it written, "Yes, there it is," I whispered aloud.

As I put the can in the basket, a spirit's caustic cackle pierced my mind, and he said, "Did you have to check the list? Poor Sharon, mind not working as well as it used to? Well, I'll help you. Let's see, time to buy vegetables. Isn't it fun shopping together?" Suddenly, his acrimony hardened to hatred, and he cursed me.

As I entered the checkout line, I greeted people, but when I smiled at the girl behind the counter, instantly I loved her, like a mother loves a daughter who pleases her. Quickly the love intensified to passion that bordered on lust. When she dropped my lettuce, a venomous rage erupted. I looked away. None of this was me.

### July 1985

"Am I hungry?" I spoke aloud to separate my thoughts from those of the spirit controlling me. "I should be. It has been four hours since breakfast." I braced for the onslaught and opened the refrigerator door. As if frozen, I stared at the whole-wheat bread and pondered aloud, "Yes, bread is nutritious, but what else would be good?" I spied the tuna and suggested, "Yes, that could be my lunch today . . . tuna and bread." I nibbled a piece of bread as I reached for the can.

"Yes, Sharon, you are hungry. You may now eat. But you cannot have tuna. Today . . . let's say . . . yes, a peanut-butter sandwich. You've had the bread. Now you may have only the peanut butter. No tuna!" Seth's voice was harsh and insistent.

Egglog, another spirit guide, defended me, "No, she likes tuna. Let her have some. Sharon, reach for the tuna and mayo." Though it no longer mattered to me what I liked or disliked, I brought the can of tuna and mayo to the counter next to the sink and opened them. Seth taunted as I willfully scooped tuna into the bowl. When I dipped my spoon into the mayo, my body filled with terror, and my head began to spin. Through the blitz, I scooped and whipped with my small salad fork until the pungent, soupy spread induced waves of nausea and I gagged.

Seth's diabolical voice pierced my mind. "I told you, no tuna! Now you must eat it all." His cursing and accusations whirled in my mind. "Wasteful! Stupid! Do you think you have money to throw around? Now eat! Eat!" I clung to the countertop, gulping air to ease the turbulence. Finally, I took a deep breath, held it, and emptied the tuna mixture down the garbage disposal. I sought refuge on my couch in the living room, as I so often did when unable to make decisions or perform simple tasks. I sat on the couch and knitted to steady my mind. I slipped the needle through the loop, wound the yarn around the tip, firmly pulled it through, and secured it in place. Yes, it looked uniform. Row upon row unfolded before me, and my mind grew still as in the eye of a hurricane, and in this respite, I experienced a bit of the person I knew myself to be. Pleased I had maintained an even pattern throughout the row, I smiled as I secured the final stitch, shifted the bulk, and began anew.

The half-completed shawl warmed my bare legs, and I welcomed the comfort of the woolen yarn in spite of the Colorado midday sun radiating behind me. The click of the needles created a cadence that lulled my mind. I savored the quiet and dared not think. The spirit seemed to delight in perverting everything about me, and I defended myself by squelching every thought, feeling, and desire.

I wrapped the strand of yarn around my finger and wove it through the loop. I had taken up knitting the year before to cope with the stress of completing my doctorate—a self-designed study that blended New Age thinking and humanistic psychology. As the professor talked, I knitted. When a concept gelled, I would push the needles through to avoid dropping a stitch, record my thoughts, and then resume my knitting. Back then the interplay of yarn and needles had counterbalanced the intellectual intensity of the classroom, but now I knitted as one clinging to a piece of wood adrift in a raging sea. The needles shuttled back and forth until the afternoon sun faded. Then I folded my shawl, and noticing how its sandy color blended with the couch, I said aloud to myself, "You remind me that goodness exists beyond this imprisonment. Like the earth, I'm connected to the whole of life. This I know to be true."

Then I saw my shadow elongated before me, and as if talking to a small child, I said, "Such a lonely, desperate figure you are. But take heart—I know you exist. Are you hungry? Never mind if you don't know. You must eat." I stared blankly at the kitchen and then whispered, "I remember liking peanut butter." The silence in my mind affirmed that I could continue thinking this way. "Yes, I like peanut butter. It would make a fine meal. I've had my bread, so I will put it on celery." I carefully put my shawl into the bag and voiced my plan. "Get a table knife and plate, peanut butter, crackers, celery, and glass of water."

The spirit lurked on the perimeter of my mind as I assembled the food and brought it to the table. I eased into the chair and gazed past my meal to the flowers in front of me. Each week I placed a fresh bouquet at the center of my round mahogany table. The sculptured glass top protected the wood surface, and tonight it reflected the flowers. Dark green ferns filled out the bouquet of pink and white carnations. I smiled. "Beauty exists in the world," I whispered, "and Starlight and many spirit angels work on my behalf."

Then my body tingled, and a flood of excitement poured through me. Starlight always announced her arrival in this way. Part of my band of spirits for over a year, she comforted me between attacks. When the spirit called Seth denied Starlight access to me, I believed that she and other spirit guides searched the spirit world for an entity with sufficient wisdom and strength to help Seth let go of me. He too could progress spiritually to a higher level of consciousness—one based on peace, love, and harmony rather than disharmony and hatred, but he had to choose it. A highly evolved entity, such as an ascended master, might be able to convince him of this. And so, I endured as Starlight and the others scouted on my behalf.

Starlight resembled an angel as she appeared in the daydreaming part of my mind. She communicated telepathically with me and said, "Oh, Sharon, the world of spirit is beautiful just beyond the dark cloud that surrounds you. Look what he's done to you! Well, the jerk is gone, so let's have fun. Let me take you on a wonderful adventure to the light. Up here it is so beautiful!"

A warm sensation washed my body, and in my mind's eye I saw a white light penetrating a vibrant purple sky. A small white dove gracefully circled the light as my body filled with joy and ecstatic waves of love. The dove soared through the expanse, and Starlight told me that she had placed my spirit on the bird, which would carry me toward the light. A bright light filled my vision as intense feelings of joy saturated me. Who could deny this experience? Then, Starlight spoke. "Yes, the light is real. Now you merely visit it, but someday you will exist in it forever."

In my vision I saw myself walking in a beautiful meadow of flowers dancing in sunlight. I heard a voice resembling mine speaking inside my mind. My spirit guides called her my higher self and told me I joined her when I slept. This spirit voice reassured me, "It's okay. You can trust Starlight. She will comfort you and warn you when the jerk comes back. Let go and enjoy!"

A tingling sensation permeated my body, and I believed my consciousness had merged with the high vibrations of the light. I had read in various New Age books that the light was the source of ultimate love. It consisted of a host of spiritual entities exuding love, peace, and power. I believed these entities had lived many lives and had learned to live in harmony with themselves and others. Some authors asserted that Jesus and Buddha were just two of the spiritual entities who existed in the light. They were models of what we all could attain. These brief visits reassured me that love and goodness existed beyond my present dilemma.

Starlight seemed as shocked as I that Seth treated me as he did. She and other spirits offered their condolences but were ineffectual against the control he exerted on my life. They assured me that they were searching the spirit realm for help and would not leave me until the situation was resolved. Though they comforted me, they fled whenever Seth returned.

And he did. Upon Seth's return I experienced first coldness and then prickling in the back of my neck followed by a suffocating depression. Terrified, I retreated to my spiritual shelf as he hissed, "If I can't feel joy, neither can you. I will not allow you to feel these things—not now or ever. Silly visions! Walks in meadows! Think that will make me leave? No one is more powerful than I, and no one can force me to release you. You are mine to do with as I please. And you will obey me.

"I'm glad you liked the peanut butter. Next time you will do as I say. I will decide what you eat, when you sleep, and what you think and feel. You will be free when I say." Seth's laughter reverberated through me as he mockingly remarked, "Maybe when I reach a higher level of consciousness I'll learn to love, but for now this is all I know to do."

The kitchen light reflected dimly off the glass of the round table, and as I stood to clear the dishes, I again saw the flowers mirrored in the tabletop. Their beauty stirred me, and for a moment my heart softened. What a tragedy: love could subdue this evil spirit, could transform him into something good, but he had to choose it.

I pleaded with him, "You don't have to be this way. Somewhere, somehow you learned to be this way, but you can learn to love. Please choose it. Try. Please try. Find an ascended master and ask him to guide you toward the light. Let go of me—for your sake! Underneath it all you are good, basically good, but the path you are on will destroy you. For your sake, let me go. Let me go!"

He feigned a whimper and whined, "Poor Seth. Poor Seth. Only knows to hurt and destroy."

I carried my empty plate, water glass, crumpled napkin, and jar of peanut butter to the kitchen. "I remember liking peanut butter as a girl," I said and then pondered, "but if I had a choice, would I have eaten it tonight?" I did not know.

# CHAPTER 2

# God Pierced the Darkness

*The thief comes only to steal and kill and destroy; I have come that they may have life, and have it to the full* (John 10:10).

*Satan's strategy was to exaggerate his power through mental and physical attacks. God made himself known amid suffering. When I reached the end of myself, God pushed through demonic dramas and gave me hope that one day I would be free.*

That night I fell asleep listening to music, and like most nights, I awakened every three hours to a barrage of cursing and taunts. Awake for two hours, asleep for three, aroused for another two, and on through the night. That night I got up. I inched my way down the dark hall toward the dimly lit living room and sat next to my knitting on the far end of the couch. My back and side rested against the earth-tone pillows, and I curled my legs underneath me. The light from the moon streamed through the branches into my living room and cast images of dancing figures on the floor in front of me. The twilight phase of sleep where dream, demon, and I merged into grotesque images frightened me most, and I welcomed the familiar—the silhouette of my round table, the stereo across the room, and the kitchen door.

These friends helped gather me together. I carefully diverted my thoughts to the dancing figures on the silver-beige rug and the glints of light on the broad leaves of my avocado plant. Quiet.

How ironic that my quest for inner peace had led me to this place. This quiet meant nothing beyond the pleasure of the moment, and I felt like a thief stealing it. Simple pleasures no longer masked the harshness of the spiritual realm, and I realized the unfolding universe was more treacherous than nurturing and could not sustain me. Where could I put my faith?

I genuinely loved the objects of my faith, and yet to date each had collapsed under scrutiny, because their foundations were insufficient to bear the weight of my life. At first, I seemed the better for it: I learned from my mistakes and turned to something more life-giving—a person, organization, or philosophy. But my journey had ended here. I was a prisoner within a body, my cell, gazing at moonbeams on a beige rug, begging for sleep, and waiting for an ascended master, a highly evolved spiritual entity, to notice my plight. What went wrong?

From the beginning I believed what was said in the New Age books and followed the instruction of my spirit guides and Donna, the medium at the spiritualist church. They all said that to grow spiritually I must open my mind, release my will, and allow the universal source of life to sustain me. Ralph Waldo Emerson said it best: "There is a guidance for each of us, and by lowly listening we shall hear the right word. . . . Place yourself in the middle of the stream of power and wisdom."[1]

"Contentment?" I whispered, staring intently at the moonlight that now, instead of quieting, punctuated the pathos

---

1    Bode and Malcolm Cowley, eds., *The Portable Emerson* (New York: Penguin Books, 1981), 192.

of my situation. "'Lowly listening'—to what? My best efforts to place myself in the middle of a stream of peace have catapulted me into the pit of hell. What went wrong?" The pathos of my situation astounded me. I was putting my hopes in the possibility that a mysterious spiritual force would happen by with sufficient wisdom, power, and desire to help me. Of all the objects of my faith, this one seemed the least plausible.

"What went wrong?" I softly asked again. "How could I be this lost? Do others know about this evil? Are they up tonight like me?" I wondered if they looked normal except for their eyes. There, instead of life, one saw empty pools, sucked dry by spiritual parasites. Who believed in such things? Or did everyone assume that such inner wars emanated from within the personality or merely from circumstance? I shuddered and asked, "How wrong was I?"

Initially my spiritual journey was fueled by a desire to find a wellspring to fill the center of me, a place to visit for nourishment. I discovered metaphysical books in the mid-seventies when I was thirty-four years old. A blend of psychology, Eastern religious thought, and more, they described a supernatural realm in which thought and energy merged in creative explosions with life-enhancing capabilities. Intrigued, I sought a laboratory in which to explore this vast mysterious realm and so joined a meditation group at a spiritualist church.

For seven years I joined with others who, like me, had the gift to see and hear spirits and sought guidance and support to develop. The class was conducted by the pastor's wife, Donna, who channeled a spirit that claimed to be an Indian girl. Both Donna and the spirit girl taught us to quiet our minds and receive spirit communication. The spirits communicated telepathically, that is, in our minds. They used words, visions and physical impressions. Our task was to receive and accurately convey what we felt, saw, and heard. The spirit girl or another member of the class would confirm what I saw by reporting a similar vision or one that elaborated on mine.

We were taught that these spirits had lived many lives on Earth and that they grew spiritually as they helped us. I had begun my explorations in the mid-seventies after reading *The Nature of Interpersonal Reality* by Jane Roberts, a medium who channeled the spirit Seth. Later, while in class, Seth appeared as a vision in my mind and introduced himself, communicating telepathically. He offered to serve as a guide for my explorations of the spiritual realm, and I accepted.

When first learning about this unseen universe, I wondered why people ignored it and reasoned that perhaps others had not inherited the gift. Perhaps they feared reprisals from friends or colleagues if they pursued such adventures in consciousness. Every morning I meditated for a half hour followed by an equal time of yoga. I sought to harmonize my soul by synchronizing my spirit with the "Universal Consciousness of All That Is." At the church and through my reading, I learned that our spirits were connected to everything, collectively contributed to All That Is, or God, Itself more than the sum of the parts. By meditating I could attain unity in my spirit and thus create love, peace, and harmony in my soul and body. Spiritual forces of darkness could not touch me. I had nothing to fear but fear itself.

I glanced out the window through branches to the moon hanging precariously in the dark, then at the shadowy dancing figures, and uncurled my legs. Walking silently down the hall, I said aloud, "He'll let me sleep." I slipped into bed, turned on my side, curled into a ball, and relaxed my mind. All was quiet. I needed no radio to blot out his voice. The spirit rarely kept me up all night. Usually he pushed me to the brink and then backed off.

Three hours later when the sun fell on my face, I opened my eyes and lay still. Within seconds Seth gripped my mind, and I sprang from bed. Willfully, I pulled the salmon-colored sheet taut and meticulously folded the ends to form a border at the head. After flipping the down comforter to the center and stroking it smooth, I fluffed the pillows into a backrest for a midday nap. I strode to the bathroom to prepare for the day as if I had somewhere to go, and midway my mind whirled with raging voices and my stomach churned. I stopped, leaned against the wall until the attack abated, and resumed my routine.

It was Sunday morning, and Michael was at his father's house. I ironed. I positioned the board in front of the copper-toned washer and dryer in the laundry area of the garden-level room, picked up a blouse, and faced my computer, which was situated on the other side of the room. Scattered beneath it were papers, my "project demonstrating excellence," a final requirement for my doctorate. "I could do that this afternoon," I thought.

Seth's voice countered, "If I let you." I would not know until I started typing.

I smoothed the collar, sprayed a mist of starch, and watched it settle into the fabric. Rolls of steam lifted off the cotton as the hot iron slowly moved from one end of the collar to the other. Satisfied, I positioned the right sleeve on the board, smoothed it out, and sprayed.

I ironed the sleeves, first the right and then the left. "That looks nice," I thought. I carelessly ironed a crease along the seam, and the spirit unleashed verbal assaults on me. I ironed through the attacks, nonsense emotions, bizarre physical sensations, and cynical interpretations of their significance. Seth played a game of infusing hateful thoughts and emotions and then castigated me for having them. For instance, when feeling tender while listening to a love song, instantly the kind of violent desire associated with rape filled my body as he attacked my character. I watched from my spiritual shelf.

The fruit of Seth's maliciousness was the perversion of every emotion, thought, and perception of myself and those I loved—present and past. He meant to meticulously destroy everything good within me. I watched his dramas like a sentinel, prepared to veto his impulses to act. Often the infusion was constant and fluctuated only in degree.

Seth's ability to do this confounded me—stripped me of everything I thought true. I had based my life on what I assumed to be fact: my inner life was my personal domain and the gist for my personal evolvement. I relied on my thoughts, feelings, and intuition to guide and fuel my personal journey. Now when I followed their lead, they spiraled me deeper into an abyss of confusion and evil.

"How long has this spirit been with me, confusing and thwarting my efforts to right the wrongs in my life? My efforts are useless—my deliverance must come from spirit." I repeated, ". . . must come from spirit."

I finished the blouse and picked up another. Then the unexpected happened. In an instant my mind became clear and a revelation pierced through to my spirit: God existed. The disclosure astounded me, and I knew it was true. Very little could penetrate the spiritual wall of evil around me, but this revelation did, and it spoke to me on my spiritual shelf. God existed. More than the synergism of all consciousness in the physical and spiritual universe, God existed as an entity separate from me and from the evil that consumed me. In an instant, I realized that God was the

One who embodied love and that God never intended me to live in this dreadful state.

I collapsed on the steps sobbing. I cried out, "You are there. You do exist. You do love me." Again, I said this, tears streaming down my face. My relief profound, I stuttered, "I know you expect me . . . to get myself out of this . . . but knowing you exist means so much . . . Thank you. Oh, thank you . . . I wish I could be with you . . . You give me hope . . . Someday I'll be safe again."

I cradled my head in my arms and soaked in the reality of God's existence and love for me. I fashioned him as a bright star in the heavens showering light and love on me, but given my present state, direct communication was impossible. Once released from this evil, I sensed that I could talk freely with my Creator.

Over the next few weeks my tenuous hold on life weakened. Knowing love existed just out of reach made my daily life more intolerable. I reasoned that since God loved me, he would not want me to live a life not my own. The decision to commit suicide seemed a pragmatic one, the most reasonable course to take given my circumstance.

I made the decision in August 1985 while walking through crowds in between events at the Aspen Music Festival. Seeing the sun-tanned, smiling faces of people lounging outside the cafés reminded me of what my life once was and could never be again while a captive of spiritual evil. Not long ago I had skied the mountain, now decorated in wildflowers, and walked with friends along the promenade, tossing my head and laughing. Now, behind dark sunglasses, tears flowed unchecked down my cheeks, and I stopped at a crosswalk, uncertain which way to go, across the street, right, left—would it matter? No, my decisions counted for nothing.

Just two hours before, I had sat on a steel folding chair, one in a row extending the width of a massive white tent set on green grass. I stared at a young girl's fingers flying up and down the keyboard as she played a familiar piano concerto. I observed a skillful technician, but the melodic strains barely penetrated the shrieking in my mind. Music, people, my will—nothing quelled the storm, that is, nothing on earth, "Oh, God, let me be close to you. It's useless. Nothing I do makes a difference. I cannot go on. I'm coming home to you."

Convinced of God's existence and the hopelessness of my situation, I intended to first talk with my son's father. I sat on the padded bench of the dojo, which was a gymnasium covered with mats. Michael squared his shoulders, broke into a run, and when at full stride, hopped and simultaneously dropped his right shoulder and tumbled head over heels to land on his feet. After the warm-up exercises, the instructor lectured the boys on the restrained use of power, and I prepared to talk with his dad. I envisioned myself saying, "Michael is at the age when I think it would be good for him to live with you. Can he move in with you before school starts, say in the next couple weeks?" I expected him to be thrilled.

Carl arrived and sat beside me as the boys formed pairs for their matches. He warmly greeted the people around us, and when he paused, I turned to look him in the eye. As I opened my mouth to speak, abruptly, all spiritual oppression ceased. My mind, body and spirit were free. Instantly, I thought, "I'm to live," Only God could do this—only a superior spiritual source could shut them up and force them to let go of me. My mind quieted for the first time in eight months. I knew that the spirits could kill me and that they wanted me dead. Someone stronger had intervened. Yes, one day I would be free. I closed my mouth, turned, and stared at Michael. His back was arched, and his face was red as he strained to resist his opponent's pin. Using his full strength and then some, he dug his heels into the mat and twisted and turned until he wrenched free. Nodding my head, I said to myself, "I will fight. I'll hold on until help comes."

Thereafter, for longer periods during the day, I could think without interruption or caustic comments. Seth assumed control when my ability to function was not essential. But I had hope that a strong, superior spiritual entity would eventually free me.

# CHAPTER 3

# Counterfeit Jesus Could Not Save Me

*And no wonder, for Satan himself masquerades as an angel of light* (2 Cor. 11:14).

*After God revealed himself, the demons manifested as biblical figures and misconstrued Scripture. The first to appear was a counterfeit Jesus.*

"FALL ON YOUR KNEES, O hear the angel voices." Tears welled up and spilled down my face as I wove through the crowded mall to the circular stage in front of the yogurt stand. Like a bird announcing the day, the soprano's voice rose above the din, and spellbound, I stood on the fringe as shoppers pressed around the platform and listened to her sing, "O night divine, O night when Christ was born!" Her black eyes glistened as she reached for the high note, ". . . di-vine," and then glided down to softly whisper, "O night divine." She sang it as if it were a love song to Jesus, and I thought my heart would burst.

I rested my hands on the wire, heart-shaped back of a chair and then eased into the seat, putting my feet under the small round table. "Led by the light of faith. . . ." The words sank into my heart and awakened a deep grief within me. "Behold your

King, before him lowly bend!" Tears poured forth as if coming from a well at the center of me, and I fumbled through my purse for a tissue, wiped my eyes, and counted change so I could buy yogurt.

I retreated from the pain by fixing my gaze on a spoonful of chocolate, and I smiled as the dark-haired soloist sang, "O come all ye faithful. . . . " Spontaneously I reminisced about how much I had loved Jesus as a child. Then he had been my trusted Friend, only a thought away; and I had hid nothing from him. At that time serious sin in my life entailed eating a second piece of fried chicken—especially the leg—before my two younger brothers and older sister had finished their first piece, not picking up the clutter in my bedroom, and being unkind to my brothers by not organizing their playtime. I brought these things to Jesus, who loved me anyway.

But God? God I feared. After church one Sunday I gleefully revealed to our pastor how my three-year-old brother had escaped from the nursery and raced through the sanctuary during the pastor's long prayer. I thought it was funny; but he sternly scolded, "Were your eyes open while we were talking to God?" His rebuke caught me off guard: Jesus loved my laughter, but God measured me with a ruler. I feared that beneath my joyful exterior, God saw an evil, selfish eight-year-old, and his punishment would be harsh.

Mother fueled my concern when she cautioned, "God blessed you with a healthy body; loving heart, and cheerful disposition, and you best put these gifts to good use." She paused and added, "Or else . . . Well, let's just say that he expects much from those he blesses." The "Or else" kindled images of the flames of hell licking my body and Satan dancing with glee as I screamed for mercy. I quivered and asked my mother, "Do bad people go to hell?"

"Let's just say you had better be a good girl and do for others!"

But with Jesus, my trusted Friend, my fears vanished. My heart swelled when I sang "Fairest Lord Jesus." I smiled, imagining Zacchaeus of Jericho climbing a fig tree to see Jesus (I would have too!), Jesus waiting patiently for me to open the door for him, and me sitting in his lap with the other children. I devoured stories about Jesus and talked to him regularly.

I circled the rim of the empty yogurt cup with my white plastic spoon. "O come let us adore him, Christ the Lord!" Covering my face with my hands, I whispered, "Oh God, I want to love again. Help me love again." I quietly admitted, "I'm a shell of a person." With my head resting in my hands, I sighed and prayed to God.

The beautiful lady bowed, and I softly clapped my appreciation. I wanted to hear more. The musicians quietly conferred with one another, and the shoppers gathered their belongings. They laughingly shuffled around the tables and around each other, picking up wrappers, spoons, and cups, and then leaving with a fresh determination to complete their lists. Tears flowed down my cheeks. Yes, I wanted more. "Go to the parking lot!" Like a startled deer I stilled my mind, straightened, and shifted my focus to the part of my mind where visions appeared. First, I saw the jeweled crown resting on his thick, unruly red hair, and then his strong, kind face turned toward me. Egglog, my primary guide, smiled confidently and, in his most paternal voice, relayed that an entity from the light had agreed to help. "You must go to the parking lot and find a secluded place. An ascended master is descending and preparing to talk with you." He paused, prompting me to express gratitude.

As if displaced from time and space, I stared blankly at him, then at the bustling crowd, and then down at my empty yogurt cup. My heart pulsated like a puncture wound as my eyes followed a line of children winding through the tables to the circular stage to sing their carols. I wanted to stay. "You are fortunate he has agreed to help," Egglog chided.

I could not afford to reject the efforts of those working to free me, and I turned my attention inward, toward the spirit realm, refocusing and simultaneously detaching from my emotions and thoughts. From this vantage point I could observe myself, not be unduly swayed. With my passions and thoughts in check, I observed myself, my surroundings, and my guides—a skill honed through years of meditating when I associated growing spiritually with detaching or transcending passions and thoughts.

I worked my way past beaming parents, the flashes on their cameras popping while their children sang, "Away in a manger, no crib for a bed, the little Lord Jesus laid down his sweet head. . . . " The well in my heart erupted as I heard songs of Jesus Christ and saw the sweetness of the children in their red velvet dresses, their faces full of hope and love. But I left because my guides directed me elsewhere.

I searched the jammed parking lot for a secluded place, and finding none, I rested against a light pole, breathed deeply, closed my eyes, and released my will. Suddenly my mind burst with color and sounds. In the vision angels emerged from the brilliance, singing and lifting their hands in adulation. A massive figure descended from clouds with bolts of white light radiating from his being. A figure resembling Jesus appeared. He extended his arms and fixed his piercing blue eyes on me.

He spoke to me telepathically, "I've come to save you—to set you free. But first I must prepare for the battle. This afternoon I will meditate to build a wall of protection, and when sufficiently fortified, I will fight this evil one. Your guide will notify you when this is to take place." Angels sang "Alleluia" as the vision faded.

A sinister laugh erupted within my mind, and Seth mocked the entourage and mimicked Jesus. In singsong cadence, he taunted, "Goody-Goody is going to take the big bad wolf and throw him into the sea!" Torrents of vulgar expletives hounded me as I searched for my car. I repeated aloud, wandering though the lot, "I can find my car, and if not, then I will sit until this passes. I can find my car." I stood still until Seth's ranting subsided, and when my mind cleared, I walked straight to my car. Exhausted, I maneuvered past the brightly decorated mall and headed home.

Would this "spirit Jesus"—the ascended master from the light—defeat this entity? I suspected not and thought it strange that an entity of his stature was attracted to my situation, especially given my rejection of him in my teens. I gave him a nod at Christmas and enjoyed the trees, packages, cards, and music. His name symbolized love and warmth—but power? How could this metaphor for love free me? Although the notion seemed preposterous, I would do as I was told.

At the appropriate hour I set the stage—lowered the lights, turned off the music, sat erect on the couch, and quieted my mind. I scarcely moved as I stared at the blackness. Suddenly my mind burst with light as a heavenly host of angels and a figure who appeared to be Jesus himself descended from billowing clouds. But Seth's cackle disrupted the drama, and Egglog, my friend and advocate, apologized and explained that the two—Jesus and my adversary—had moved outside my vision to do battle. I heard the clashing and mashing of bodies, moans, screams of pain, and shouts of victory, and then quiet. As if from a distant field, I heard the steps of the victor coming to claim his bounty. A raucous hilarity filled my mind and then an eerie quiet. Seth whispered, "The wimp is no match for me!"

I was Seth's captive. Albeit unwittingly, I had become a pawn in a spiritual battle and was utterly ignorant of my enemy and his terrain, weapons, and rules of warfare. Not knowing what else to do, I reached for my knitting. Row after row my fingers pushed the large needle through the loop, hooked the strand around the point, and pulled the yarn through. These simple strokes had produced a beautiful shawl. I gazed at the Christmas tree adorned with angels, white lights, and bulbs.

I spied a strand of tinsel encircling the neck of a white ceramic angel and said aloud, "Tinsel is a suitable necklace for a messenger of love! But you promise much and deliver little!" Weary, as if my core had been pared away, I whispered to the angel, "Your insides are hollow like mine. Is anything as it seems? Would God create me and leave me prey to evil spirits with no protection or provision? Where is my hope? Or is this vacancy at the center of me a permanent condition and this torture a life sentence? But for what? Why?" Adamantly I rushed to my defense, "I've done nothing to deserve this treatment. Nothing!"

Since my early childhood I had tried to ask no more from others than what they could freely give. In therapy I learned about the influence of my upbringing and worked to correct the self-defeating behaviors and thoughts. When I realized that my efforts to improve my relationships and inner life could not fill the vacancy deep within my soul, I turned to the spiritual. I vigorously sought to understand the dimensions of its influence and my responsibility in improving conditions within me and in the world. My sincerity or genuineness could not be faulted, nor could the motivation for my striving. A hunger deep inside had demanded satiation, and I trusted the spirits to help me address this need. They had helped me before, when I first communicated with them as a young girl.

### Early Years

Through the years, my father had told me of the conditions in my family before my birth. He always began by saying, "You were an answer to prayer." Then his eyes clouded as he described how my sister died three years before my birth. "In 1939, medical supplies were scarce in the small Missouri town where your mother and I lived with five-year-old Sandra and two-year-old Jackie Jo. Both girls were sick, but the fever ravaged Jackie Jo's body. In a desperate attempt to save her life, the doctor ordered a blood transfusion. She died within a couple days."

My dad cleared his throat before continuing. "Through it all she never cried or complained. . . . What a beautiful angel!" My dad's eyes grew misty at this point in the story. "I watched my blood flow into her arm, but I knew it was wrong to do. I had B-negative blood and she had O-positive, . . . but I was desperate! I think it killed her. I think my blood killed her." He asked me with his eyes, "Do you understand? I didn't mean to kill her. Do you forgive me? Can you make it better?"

I diverted my gaze.

My parents prayed and said that three years later God gave them a baby girl, a replica of the one lost. They looked at my face, saw hers instead, and instinctively loved me. Later I mistook her baby picture for mine, but Mother laughed and assured me I had more vinegar in my system than my sister had had.

Although my parents looked to God to redeem their situation, I knew they feared him. Instead of seeing God as loving and just, they perceived him to be capricious—prone to fits of temper, cruelty, and random acts of kindness. Would he take this child too? As a result, they loved both God and me from a distance.

When I was three years of age, spirit playmates joined me. I talked to them in my mind, and they never left my side, even during meals. My mother placed four white plates at one end of the kitchen table, where I sat tall and placed a pea in the center of each. Totally absorbed in feeding lunch to my spirit friends, I laughed and said aloud that they must eat their vegetables. Mother often let them eat with me, but she insisted that they existed only in my imagination. I knew differently. I saw and heard them as clearly as I saw and heard her. I talked with Bobo, Me-me, and Fifi in my mind and sometimes aloud, but I was the only one who perceived them. My special friends and I stayed out of the way, bothering no one, as we pretended to ride powerful black horses, played games, and entertained my younger brother and mother. They made me laugh.

Bobo was a mischievous boy who loved taking me on wild adventures. Sweet Me-me encouraged me to help my family and be kind. Fifi, a beautiful angel, told me the secrets of people around me. She helped me understand others, why they behaved as they did and what they felt. She comforted me. I loved them all very much. We liked to play outdoors, and one day while in the front yard, Bobo darted into the street. A car spun from nowhere, and I watched, terrified, as Bobo collapsed under the tire. I ran screaming to my mother. Soon after, Me-me and Fifi came to play less and less.

My family began attending a Presbyterian church, and as the spirits disappeared, Jesus Christ came into my life. He became my refuge, my port in the storm. Jesus never appeared to me in visions as the other spirits had, but we communicated nonetheless, and I trusted him to take care of me. The Sunday school teachers encouraged me to pray to Jesus, so I talked to him throughout the day.

We lived in a large white house surrounded by apple trees and perched on a hill in the bluffs of western Wisconsin. My mother managed the household of four children, a dog, cat, and many broods of kittens. My father traveled for a family owned business, coming home two weekends a month.

The trees were my sanctuary and the hills a playground as my imagination provided the fodder for play. As a seven-year-old, I often pretended to be a horse. Tingling with excitement, I pawed the air, shook my black mane in the sunlight, and neighed at my five-year-old brother, Tom, to alert him to rein me toward our neighbor's real-life stallion, Babe. The rope clinched tightly in my mouth, I responded to the tug, and we galloped across the road.

We stopped at the driveway and scanned the barnyard for Mr. Benson before climbing the fence to pet the monstrous black plow horse. Mr. Benson's warning echoed in our minds: "Never enter the pasture. Those horses are for work, not play." Standing on the top rung of the fence, we waved our carrots and neighed, "We have carrots! Come let us pet you!" Babe feigned indifference but slowly ate his way toward the fence. At last we stroked his sleek, black side, and I whispered, "I love you Babe, my beautiful stallion." I rested my head on his broad back and inched aboard. Straddling my steed, I scarcely heard Mr. Benson scream, "Get off that horse!" as he ran toward us down the long driveway.

"Sharon, get off!" Tom shouted.

I slid down the belly of the horse, crawled under the fence, and straightened my shoulders to receive Mr. Benson's tongue-lashing. Although clearly concerned, the twinkle in his blue eyes betrayed him as he threatened, "I'll haul you to your mother by your ears if you don't scoot on home. Never enter the pasture.

Those horses are for work, not play!" We bolted across the road and hid in the sanctuary of our apple orchard.

Here I talked with Jesus, "Dear Jesus, I'm sorry I disobeyed. No matter how much I love Babe, I know I'm not to get on his back. Please forgive me, and make Mr. Benson like me again." I trusted Jesus to take care of me, and I always felt better after one of our talks.

Dolores lived next door to me, and though she was six years older than I, we played together and sometimes I worked alongside as she did her chores. As a nine-year-old, I loved being with her because she told stories as we shined the stainless steel sink, wiped the floor, loaded the washing machine. Enthralled, captivated, I listened as she told her tale.

My friend's eyes widened when she told a Cinderella story of how the dark-haired beauty gracefully followed the lead of the prince, "Her dress, which fit snug to the waist and then flared, brushed his legs as they whirled. . . . " I put myself into her story, dancing and swishing as the prince guided me around the ballroom.

Dolores stepped back to admire our handiwork.

"Are we finished?" I asked, wanting to play with the paper dolls tucked under her bed.

"No, not yet. Mother said to wipe the floor, dust the living room, make the beds, and start the laundry. Then we play."

Later my mother asked, "You mean you go there to help Dolores clean? You could do that here, you know."

"It's more fun to wash a stainless sink; it shines when you're done," I said. But really, I worked alongside Dolores because she made work more like play.

My mother held a clothespin in her mouth as she stretched a sheet down the line, and once it was taut, she deftly stuck the pin at the comer's edge. "Hand me another," she instructed. She put two more pins in her mouth, smoothed the corner over the line, stuck it with a pin, and pulled the rest down the line. With one basket hung, she returned to the washing machine and threaded the next load through the wringer piece by piece. She looked sad as she rested her weary arms on the sink, sighed, and carried the basket to the line. She had four children, and doing the laundry took all day.

She said, "Last week I heard that Dolores' mother was pretty hard on her for coming home five minutes late from a date."

"Dolores is going to be a nun, Mom."

"Yes, I know. But she is fifteen."

"I guess so, but why would a nun want to be with a boy?" Dolores had explained that when she became a nun, Jesus Christ would be her husband, and I could no longer call her Dolores. In fact, I would not be able to see her, perhaps for years, while she learned how to please him. Privately I considered her the most Christian person I knew: She saw the best in people, never complained or put herself first, joyfully obeyed her parents, and laughed in the most trying situations. Incredible! Every Lent I proved my love to Jesus by giving up eating chocolate, chewing gum, and biting my nails. I lasted a half day before gnawing a nail, and I held out a week before buying an ice cream bar. Burning with guilt, I reckoned that chewing gum could hardly worsen my standing with God.

But Dolores was different. Whether shining stainless steel, sweeping the floor, or discussing her plans to marry Jesus Christ, I sensed she pleased God. I tried to be like her. Cathy, a Catholic girl my own age, boasted, "It's fine if I lie to my grandmother today, because tomorrow I'm going to confession. We Catholics get to do that." I nodded, but could not imagine Dolores saying that.

"Hey! I'll let you sit on a pew at my church," Cathy once said mischievously.

Horrified, I countered, "Oh, no, I couldn't!"

"No, it's fine. The priest is off today. Come on!" she yelled and motioned me to follow as she ran toward the church.

"Cathy, wait for me!" I screamed, scampering behind.

We tiptoed up the marble steps and opened the double doors. When my eyes adjusted to the light, I saw Cathy vanishing through the next set of tall doors; I stopped dead still. Cathy had often brandished her rosary with the silver crucifix dangling at one end to gain some advantage, but never had I seen a crucifix as awesome as the one in front of me now. I stepped back to look full at Jesus hanging on a cross, floor to ceiling, on the yellow-beige, marble wall. Blood dripped from punctures inflicted by the thorny crown smashed onto his head; it trickled down the silent suffering I saw etched in Jesus' face. His head slumped to one side, almost touching his shoulder, and his arms were stretched out, secured with nails hammered through his palms. More blood oozed. His body, once writhing in pain, now hung limp, knees bent, propped by crossed feet embedded with more nails. I remembered that my pastor had said, "Jesus died for you, and you're to lay down your life for him." Like Dolores? I wondered. I stared at the dying Jesus as if expecting him to raise his head and answer me.

"Psst," Cathy interrupted, "they're this way! The pews I said you could sit on, they're in here."

Marble statues of robed men lined the sanctuary on both sides, and down front, off to the side, I spied the breathtaking figure of Mary, her arms reaching as if to hold me. My heart pounded at the awe-filled majesty of God's house, and then terror hit! Does God punish impostors—those pretending to be Catholic but who are really Protestant?

"Let's get out of here!" I whispered, "I'm going to get caught!"

"No, I'll tell the priest you're a Catholic. Come sit down and tell me if they're different from Protestant pews." She crooked her finger, and when I hesitated, she encouraged, "Don't worry. This is not a mortal sin, you know. Anyway, tomorrow I go to confession."

"You going to confession won't do me much good, and I want outta here!" I bolted from the church and headed for Cathy's house. Her giggles told me she was close behind.

I imagined running smack into a man dressed in black with a thin white collar, a crucifix dangling from his neck—the holiest of the holy—the last person a Protestant wanted to see when sneaking into a Catholic church.

As a child I trusted Jesus, but my heart broke during my teenage years and my childlike faith collapsed. I deemed the stories of Jesus more mythical than true and categorized Christianity alongside Santa Claus and other myths and fables. I decided that belief in Jesus could hardly serve as the foundation for my life.

"Is anything as it seems?" I mused, staring at the tiny white lights illuminating the angel atop my  tree. Suspended beneath her, two cherubs swayed slightly while the tinsel encircling their bodies reflected glints of light. These symbols of love, metaphors of peace, still warmed my heart. "What an idealist I am, what a dreamer! Why do I continue to hope?" I wondered. And yet I did continue to hope.

The next day the spirit Jesus appeared in a vision to apologize for his failure. He came without fanfare and advised me, "Your guides must leave, but I will stay to give you whatever encouragement I can. They will now say good-bye."

Egglog came first. "Your situation has worsened, and in all good conscience, I must allow others the opportunity to help you. I wish you the best."

I said, "I'm sure it has been hard on you, and through it all you've been respectful and kind to me. I thank you for your patient guidance. I've learned so much. Don't worry about me. I'll be fine." They came one by one to reminisce and to offer condolences for the condition of my life and best wishes for the future. Although I had communicated with them for eight years, I felt nothing for them. They smiled and vanished.

Over the next few months, whenever alone, I listened politely as "Jesus" and his disciples told me the real story of his life. Totally uninterested, I wondered for whose benefit they narrated the most obscure details of his life and ministry. None of it resembled what was recorded in the Bible.

# CHAPTER 4

# They All Lied!

*There is a way that appears to be right, but in the end it leads to death* (Prov. 14:12).

*Finally, the house of cards collapsed, and I saw that every spirit was evil. The wisdom they preached was foolishness. None reflected the way God designed, sustained, and ruled His universe.*

MICHAEL HAD JUST LEFT FOR school, and I appreciated the quiet within my mind as I finished my breakfast. I ate the last piece of shredded wheat and sat back in my chair. During the last ten years I had systematically eliminated sugar, red meat, caffeine, and alcohol from my diet in an effort to better care for myself. Periodically I cleansed my body of impurities by withholding all food for ten days, drinking only water and juice from raw fruits and vegetables. My body resembled that of a teenager's, standing five feet two inches tall and weighing 112 pounds. Throughout the year or so of spiritual harassment, I had lost six pounds, and each day I made sure my body received the nourishment it needed. Fruit, raw vegetables, whole grains, fish and poultry, brown rice, skim milk, and lots of water were my staples.

My body felt lithe, a little otherworldly. Through the day I would spontaneously stroke an arm, rub my stomach, caress my face, or wrap my arms around myself for reassurance. I was absolutely still. Nothing moved. No thoughts. No past or future. Nothing but the quiet. Here I rested.

Starlight came first. I had not seen her in three months, since my former guides had said good-bye and the spirit Jesus and his band of disciples became my primary helpers. This morning Starlight announced herself in the usual way with a rush of excitement followed by laughter and joyous singing. I closed my eyes and immediately saw her dressed in white with light beams streaming from her gown and merging with a background of sparkling stars. She looked splendid!

But in a blink of an eye her persona changed. A gargoyle, baring razor-sharp teeth, opened and closed his mouth and spit streams of fire at me. An eerie film covered bulging eyes that stared at me through vacuous holes where pupils should have been. His head thrust toward me, recoiled, and then sprang again to spew his hatred.

Suddenly he disappeared, and next I saw the back of Egglog's head. His unruly red hair, topped with a jeweled crown, slowly turned, and he spoke in a kind, authoritative tone so familiar to me, "Sharon, we've come to check on you and to see if your situation has been resolved." But when he faced me, he appeared as an ever-changing amoebic mass, spitting venom and bile. Quickly, he disappeared.

The spirit Jesus, his disciples, and every spirit I had ever known came first in their splendor and then as grotesque instruments of evil. In an instant, I knew an awful truth: for the past ten years I had been duped by evil entities masquerading as spirit guides, wise counselors, deceased relatives, saints, and angels. They had dazzled me with their prowess and noble thoughts, camouflaging their sadistic nature and sinister designs for my life.

"All evil! I can trust none of them! What will I do?" I talked aloud to differentiate my voice from theirs. Clinging to the edge of the table, I pleaded with myself, "Don't panic. You'll find a way. Walk! Start walking!"

I circled the living room and deliberately looked at the floor, the couch, the blue sky, and back to the floor, all the while speaking aloud to override the pandemonium within my mind. "Focus on what is real—the couch, the plant, the sky. These things are real. The others are all liars. Listen to none of it. Never again acknowledge their presence!" I continued pacing and reassuring myself, "I do exist separate from them, and I will find a way to get free. Now keep walking!"

As I paced from room to room, I began pleading, "God, help me. Please, God, help me." I walked, prayed, and talked to myself as the spirits spun my mind and inflicted sharp pains throughout my body. I walked faster and talked louder and then bolted through the front door and half jogged down the street. I stopped to touch the earth, finger a rock, watch the cars, and observe my neighbors removing sticks and winter debris from their yards.

Then my mind quieted. Much like a waif rummaging through rubble, I picked my way through the deathly still, and as I did, I realized that a force more cunning and heinous than I could fathom had systematically set out to deceive and destroy me. I said to myself, "I can't know the extent of their power and wickedness, but I must live as if they are not here. I will never again talk to them, either mentally or verbally, and will deny all thoughts and feelings that do not resemble how I remember myself to be. I would rather live a life of silence than allow them to use me for their purposes. I must learn how to do this."

I sat down on the front steps of my home and fixed my gaze on the cottonwood tree spreading its arms into the blue sky before me. Terror crept into my body, and then the demons' whisperings invaded my mind. Reflexively I mouthed, "Sharon, take hold. Don't indulge this feeling or these voices. It's not you. You will find a way. Now look at the tree." The first branch jutted five feet above the ground, and others followed one on top of the other. The upper ones paralleled the roof of my house. My heart pounded. I spied strands of cassette tape dancing in the March wind. It draped over the branches, obvious remnants from the escapades of the neighborhood kids last fall when they had tossed it, as well as toilet paper, into all the trees up and down the block. Of course, the wind and snow had whisked the paper away, but the thin brown film wound around and clung to the branches with the tenacity of a snake.

"How am I going to get that down?" I asked myself. My skin tingled, sweat trickled down my sides, and my stomach knotted as feelings of dread permeated my body. "Take deep breaths. It means nothing," I said and shifted my attention. "Perhaps I could borrow an extension ladder, or maybe I can hook it with a rake. It's worth a try." The whisperings of the chorus in my head reached a crescendo as I carried a rake from the garage and hoisted it up the tree.

Seth taunted, "Never. Never will this work, you stupid thing. Now let us help you figure this out. You'll never be able to do it on your own!" I ignored him, but indeed the handle was too short, and as I lowered it, he instructed, "Now, you know who did this, and you must correct them. Go find them and tell them to clean up their mess. Do it now!" My heart hardened, and rage erupted within me as he hissed, "Give them what they deserve."

I retreated to the front step and stared helplessly at the bare branches and the film dancing against the brilliant blue backdrop. I told myself, "Do nothing. No matter what, never express his viciousness. This isn't you nor your way of dealing with people. The tape can stay there all summer if need be. It doesn't matter. These spirits may be able to make you think and feel, but you can reject what they say and deny them expression in your life. Just do your best. That's all you can do."

That day I said, "Ignore. Retreat. They lie. Deny them," but ten years earlier I had related to them much like a child taking her first steps toward her mother's outstretched arms. Why? Because I believed that laws governed the spiritual universe and protected me from harm. "Like attracts like," the authors and leaders said. "When you seek after truth and love, you attract spiritual energies of a like nature, and they empower your journey." I believed them. I thought that as I pursued spiritual truths, the universe facilitated my development and nothing of a lower or unlike nature could harm me. I first learned these principles while reading the Seth books.

Whenever I picked up Seth's books, the rest of my life faded away as if someone had flipped a switch inside of me. I could not even say why or how it happened or what captivated me, but as I read *Seth Speaks* and *The Nature of Interpersonal Reality* by the medium Jane Roberts, the words on the page jumped out at me, and I felt alive. Seth, the spirit she channeled and the supposed author of the book, painted a word picture of his life in spirit and the relationship of his world to ours.

I read about such things in a room my husband and I had converted to a library. In the center stood a black octagonal fireplace that warmed the main floor of our mountain home during the winter months. The fireplace dominated the room, which was carpeted with a moss-green, short shag rug. A huge dark brown plush chair and a floor-to-ceiling bookshelf sagging with books furnished the room. Opposite the bookshelf was a window seat covered with houseplants short enough to allow a full view of the redwood deck, evergreen trees, and mounds of snow.

However beautiful the world outside, I was happy to be on this side of the glass, warmed by the fire, my book in hand, and curled in the plush brown chair. Weekly I retreated to this place— away from the intensity and demands of my private practice and responsibilities as a wife and as a mother of an eight-month-old. During these times, I addressed a deep personal need.

The yearning to explore my spirituality overtook me shortly after the birth of my son in 1976. With my life so well situated I could afford to explore this aspect of my life. It was as if something within me picked me up and shifted my focus away from psychology toward concerns of a spiritual nature. Despite my professional and personal accomplishments, a gnawing pulled at me from deep inside. I awakened to an emptiness deep in my core and decided that it signaled a spiritual lack. I set out to research the possibilities with the same boldness with which I had approached all else in my life.

"Fascinating!" I uttered half aloud as my thoughts exploded, "What Seth says coincides with psychology and yet takes it to a new level. He too believes that people live a fraction of their potential, but he adds that spirit can empower us as we journey toward actualization. I wonder how that works?"

"What did you say?" My husband inquired as he passed through the room. "What are you reading?"

"It's a fascinating book about spiritual development, and the author offers a perspective I've not heard before. He says that everything in nature has a spirit that interacts and contributes to the evolution of life. He refers to God as 'All That Is'—I guess because God is like a compilation of all spiritual energies."

His curiosity piqued, he stopped and asked, "That is interesting. What else does he say?"

"Well, . . . that we can learn to focus our spirit, or consciousness, through meditation practices, and that spiritual energy systems empower us as we tap into them."

"Hey, tell it to zap me as I plow the driveway. It looks like the Arctic out there," he laughed.

"No, really, what he says is completely compatible with existential philosophy and humanistic theories. He says that we are responsible for how we manage ourselves, but he adds that our spirit is linked to a vast spiritual universe containing pockets of power and wisdom. He says we communicate with it, and it with us, through intuition, dreams, visions, and meditative states." I paused and added, "I guess spirits have a perspective quite different from ours."

"And ours may be skewed!" He added, "Reminds me of the story of ten blind men trying to describe an elephant. The one holding the tail says it's long and skinny, another one insists it's shaped like a trunk, and the; one stroking the stomach. . . . Well, you know what I mean."

"Yes, and maybe because spirits reside in another dimension and yet have lived many lives here, they are better able to see the whole of life. We only see the parts. Perhaps we're surrounded by a vast spiritual universe waiting for us to explore. Wouldn't that be fun? Could be an adventure. What do you think?"

Shaking his head, he turned and teased, "I think it still looks like the Arctic out there, and I'll leave it to you to figure out the inner truths of the universe while I go plow this one." Before the doors closed behind him, I was once again engrossed in my book and read until the room grew dark. "Time to resume my life," I sighed and reluctantly put the book down. Still hungry for more information, I wondered if anyone in the Denver area knew about this. Then I remembered that Jane Roberts had initially contacted Seth while experimenting with a Ouija board, and I decided to follow her example.

That week I bought a Ouija board, and the following Saturday afternoon I watched my hands involuntarily move the pointer from letter to letter across the board. Gradually words and then sentences formed. During the next couple hours, a spirit introduced himself by spelling his name and describing details of his life before he died. Mesmerized, I asked him questions by moving the pointer from one letter to another, and he answered in the same manner. But toward the end of the afternoon, he responded to questions before I spelled them on the board—as they formed in my mind!

My experience supported the beliefs of Jane Roberts. Indeed, a spiritual universe coexisted with ours, and persons who had once lived on earth now resided in a dimension outside the confines of time and space. Could Seth be right about the rest? Eager and thrilled, I waited for the universe to lead me further. I did not wait long.

# CHAPTER 5

# The Deceit of Divination

*When someone tells you to consult mediums and spiritists, who whisper and mutter, should not a people inquire of their God? Why consult the dead on behalf of the living?* (Isa. 8:19).

*I was mesmerized by visions and spirits, who became my authority on spiritual matters. No wonder God hates the practice!*

IN 1977, I CONDUCTED A private practice in marriage and family therapy. One day a client opened her session by stammering, "I visited a . . . uh . . . a medium. I hope you don't think me crazy. My family has consulted Donna for years. She goes into a trance, and a spirit girl speaks through her. I mean the spirit uses Donna as her instrument so that she can talk to us from the spirit world." Marilee glanced at me and laughed, "Sounds silly, huh? I know a lot of people scoff at such things."

"Oh, I'm open," I said warmly. "Please continue. I don't think less of you, Marilee, for consulting a medium. What did this lady tell you?"

In one hour the spirit had summarily identified Marilee's symptoms, the source of her problem, and how to resolve it. "How did she do that, Marilee? We've been working on this for six months, and in one hour she has it all figured out! How much information did you give her?"

"Really none at all. I simply sat down, and she started talking. She is amazing! I'm glad you don't think I'm weird."

"Like I said, I make no judgments about these matters. I think every person has the right, even the responsibility; to explore the spiritual dimension of life wherever that might lead. In fact, I'm beginning to believe that the universe provides the right 'teacher' for each step of our journey, and it's our job to keep our eyes and ears open." I smiled and continued, "Who am I to say what's right for you? No one knows more about the purpose and conditions in your life than you! So, I encourage you to determine right thought and action based on your experience and situation. . . . Believe in yourself and do whatever you sense you must do." I invited her to continue.

Spellbound, I listened to my client's tales. This spirit girl seemed to have an uncanny ability to parse an issue and occasionally predict the outcome of complex situations. "She's not a hundred percent accurate, but she's good! Donna's home is near your office. You should give her a call," Marilee said as she gathered her belongings and prepared to leave.

I closed the door behind her and thought, "My, that didn't take long! Last week the Ouija board and now this. What stronger confirmation do I need?" My insides lit up like a Christmas tree. I made an appointment.

"Come in, the door is open!" a man yelled from inside the house just as I raised my hand to knock. My heart raced, and I thought, "It's one thing to read about psychics and quite another to actually open the door!" I grabbed the cold knob and pushed the door open.

The man continued, "Something's wrong with this knee . . . swells something terrible if I'm up too long. Works best if I keep it elevated for a couple hours in the afternoon. . . . Hey, come on in!" Once my eyes adjusted to the dimly lit room, I saw a stout, gray-headed man lounging on a brown vinyl recliner. He said, "Excuse me, but I'm stuck here 'cause of this leg. Here to see Donna?" He grinned broadly and motioned me across the room, "Over there. You can sit over there on the small couch."

Sit where? I thought. Plant vines wove their way over and under piles of magazines and around frames without pictures and pictures without frames wedged between boxes of books. A maroon afghan hung from a broken chair. I politely asked, "Where would you like me to sit?"

"Oh," he laughed, "I'm John, Donna's husband. Please excuse the clutter. We never seem to get this place straightened up. Steady stream of people comes through here. Keeps Donna busy. And with my health and all. . . . Afraid it don't look as neat as the houses of the uptown folk," he laughed, "but we sure help a lot of people. Oh, sit over there. And tell that mangy cat to get down. Thinks he owns this place. Why, we've had him for more years than I can remember."

Stories poured forth from the man as I jostled the yellow tom off the settee and gently removed a stack of flowered dishes from the faded red cushion onto the floor next to a lamp that was missing its shade. Once settled, I searched my appointment book for scratch paper to record my questions. Now to prepare for my meeting, I thought.

"Number one," I wrote, "Seth says that energies of a like nature are attracted to each other. Is this true? I mean, do you cloister with spirits who have evolved to a similar level of personal development?"

"Number two. When you resolve certain issues, are you aware of moving from one level of consciousness to another as Seth describes? And then do you find yourself within a different energy system and with new spirit beings?"

John's chatter broke through, "You see, I'm the pastor at a spiritualist church here in Denver. Yep, lots of interesting things happen there. How did you hear of us?"

"From a friend. I've not been to your church." I looked past him to a cluttered dining room. Christmas wrapping paper, clothing boxes, books, and folded tablecloths, towels, sweaters, and shirts blanketed the tabletop. A dusty white crocheted tablecloth fell midway to the floor where more boxes, bulging with clothes and stacked two deep, created a path to the kitchen and to a closed door at the back of the house. "Must be where Donna sees people," I thought. My heart quickened at the thought, and my hands grew clammy. I returned to my task. "Number three. When we sleep, do our spirits communicate with other spirits?"

"Lots of needy people in this world," John loudly interjected. "Most of this stuff is left over Christmas donations for the needy donated by our church. Sure be nice to get it delivered."

I nodded, smiled, and continued writing. "Number four. When we die, where do our spirits go? Number five. What is my primary purpose for this incarnation? What lesson am I presently working through?"

As I stuffed my notepad into my appointment book, two women emerged from the back room. The younger one passed by me and let herself out the front door. The older of the two stopped at the table to move a box from one end to the other and then paused to rub her neck and raise her stooped shoulders. Pleasantly attired in a pale blue printed dress, a gray hand-knit sweater, and fuzzy bedroom slippers with leather soles, she shuffled toward me.

I stared into tired eyes. I saw no malice, no ill will. She smiled kindly and offered me her hand.

"Would you like a cup of hot tea?" she asked.

I shook her hand and replied, "Yes, that would be nice." Donna motioned for me to follow her to the kitchen.

"Someday I'll take care of this," she apologized as we passed through the dining room. "People at church gave so generously, the least I can do is organize it for others to deliver. Can't believe it's February already." Her manner disarmed me, and I suspected she had already given too much. She sighed and said, "We meet back here."

I sat in an overstuffed beige chair just inside the door, not four feet from Donna's recliner, which was pushed against the wall opposite me. With my steaming cup teetering on the arm and my notepad in my lap, I watched Donna put a small pillow decorated with maroon, white, and blue flowers behind her back. As if embarking on a marvelous adventure, I waited for her to signal our beginning.

"In a few minutes I will go into a trance and the spirit girl will speak to you. Feel free to ask her questions. After an hour I will come back, and you will again be speaking to me." She took a long sip of water and wryly explained, "She is a talker, and my mouth gets dry."

Donna closed her eyes, lifted her shoulders, wrinkled her face, and shook her head. Suddenly her face brightened, and in an animated voice that matched her new demeanor, the spirit girl welcomed me. "My, don't you have pretty colors around you today—the whites, purples, and reds radiate from your spirit. Pretty. Yes, a real pretty aura. A real dynamo you are! Yes, and I see you've brought with you two spirit guides who wish to make contact with you. . . . A healer. Yes, you help people. Yes, you

work with people . . . like as a counselor or something like that."
Transfixed, I listened as she rattled off information about me and
about my husband, son, and home.

"How do you do this?" I asked during a brief pause. "I mean,
how do you know my past, present, and future? Is it true, as
Seth suggests, that because you transcend time and space of the
physical universe, you can see things we can't? It seems that, with
your capabilities, you could really help people. May I ask you
some questions?"

The spirit girl bristled, "Well, a philosopher I'm not, but
since you have a curiosity about such things, your guides inform
me that they are willing to help. In fact, they've been waiting
for you to ask." After a long silence, she warmly offered, "Yes,
you may join our spiritual development class at the church. My
instrument, Donna, and her husband, John, are the pastors. There
you will learn to meditate and speak directly to your guides about
these matters. I'm afraid these philosophical questions are out of
my league. It's better that they guide your spiritual development."
She again paused and offered, "You are naturally gifted, and with
training you could make a fine medium. Talk to Donna about the
class. Good-bye for now. See you in class."

Donna squinted her eyes, lowered her head, and shook it from
side to side. She raised and lowered her shoulders, readjusted the
pillow in the small of her back, and slowly leaned against the back
of her recliner. Rubbing the back of her neck, Donna opened her
eyes and said, "Quite the talker, isn't she?" She reached for the
glass of water and shyly asked me if the visit went well. "Do you
have questions?"

"Where do you go when the spirit girl talks?"

"Oh, I spend time with my mother in spirit," she said. "We
walk in a meadow, and I enjoy myself."

"She mentioned that I could attend your spiritual development class. I'd like to know when and where you meet and what happens."

"We'd be happy to have you. The purpose of the class is to grow spiritually. I begin the class with exercises and a teaching, and then the spirit girl comes through to help you communicate with spirit. We meet Tuesday evenings from 6:30 until 9:30. We try to get out on time, but she gets long winded!" Donna said affectionately.

I smiled, sensing that Donna liked her, and I realized that I did too. I said, "Thank you for your help. I do appreciate your willingness to see me, and I look forward to being with you in class."

Two weeks later I joined the group of twenty or so regulars with whom I would meditate for the next seven years. We sat in folding chairs arranged in a circle, filling two-thirds of a rectangular room in the church basement. The chairs and the dark hardwood floors reminded me of my childhood Sunday school classrooms. There were other similarities—the camaraderie within the group, the Holy Bible and hymnals on the piano, and the gentle nature of our teacher, Donna. She sat in the same place each week, under the light at one end of the circle. She placed a small wooden table in front of her, on which she put her teaching aids.

Each class followed the same sequence. After Donna completed her announcements and introduction of new members, we adjusted the dimmer switch to allow a sufficient glow so as to see one another and simultaneously be aware of visions and movement of spirit as we completed our opening exercise. Then Donna gave a short teaching followed by meditation.

The spirit girl taught the remainder of the class. Serving as an intermediary between the spirit world and us, she helped us discern spirit communication from our imagination and taught us to interpret what we saw, felt, and heard. Over the years she introduced me to my five guides, who in turn worked with me in the classes. I felt their presence throughout the week, but as far as I could tell, they did not intrude into my daily life unless invited.

One night Donna introduced psychometry as the opening exercise. "Tonight we are going to practice giving readings from a personal object. Hand an item to the person seated next to you." I exchanged my bracelet for Lynn's ring. "Now close your eyes and pay attention to the images that form in your mind's eye and to the sensations in your body. The spirits have a special lesson in store for us tonight." As I held the ring in my hand, I sensed the presence of my guide, Egglog. His brightly jeweled crown and red mane took form in my day-dreaming eye. As he slowly turned toward me, he communicated mind to mind. "I will be with you tonight and lead you through this exercise." I smiled, and his face vanished.

Brilliant red lights filled the screen in my mind and then faded to a murky blue. It suddenly transformed to a cotton-like substance that thinly veiled a black expanse. Suddenly my heart exploded into a wild pounding in my chest. It skipped a beat and then gradually resumed its normal cadence. My body flushed, and in my mind's eye I saw a white light break through the black curtain. My body relaxed, and a sense of peace washed over me. Tears of joy filled my eyes. I immediately sensed that Lynn was concerned for a family member who struggled with a heart condition and that although the irregular heartbeat had caused some physical discomfort, the condition would shortly be corrected. Just as the light broke through the black curtain, so the heart would be healed, and her fear removed. I mentally thanked Egglog for the reading.

I recounted my experiences and interpretation to the class. Tearfully, Lynn verified that her uncle struggled with an irregular heartbeat. She, in turn, said to me, "This bracelet was given to you by a good friend who cared for you very much. His first name starts with a T." I nodded and confirmed that his name was Tim.

Donna continued the lesson. "Once you achieve a receptive, meditative state, spirits impress messages upon you. They use your feelings, physical sensations, visions, and intuition, and it's your job to remember and interpret what you feel, see, hear, and sense. Even if you don't understand the significance of a particular communication, report it anyway. Spirits work with the person you're reading for and further interpret your message directly to that person. Your task is to get out of the way. We want your mind to be a blank slate to enable spirits to more accurately convey their images and impressions. Practice clearing your mind and releasing your will as you meditate each morning." She looked at each member and reverently added, "Of course the purist form of communication occurs in trance, which some of you will learn to do. But don't be discouraged if you are not one of those chosen; you can still be very helpful to people." She paused, rapidly blinked her eyes, and said, "The spirit girl has something she wants to say."

Abounding with energy, she challenged, "Now, why do we do this? We in spirit communicate through images, which better describe the whole of a situation than, say, the way you think, all logical and in a straight line. You are forced to use sentences and logical sequences of thought while we in spirit capture the whole of the situation. Any questions?"

Members of the class engaged in a lively debate, interspersed with laughter and teasing. At the close of the class, the spirit girl said, "Hopefully some of you will allow your guides to use you as their instruments."

She looked directly at me! But what more could I do to prepare myself? I meditated and performed yoga for an hour each morning, read voraciously about spiritual matters, and attended class religiously. My husband said that my preoccupation with spiritual development had become an obsession, and indeed it had! But what a wonderful obsession!

For several mornings during my hour-long meditations, I experienced tender, loving feelings as a delicate flower appeared in my mind's eye. I asked the instructor about it during class, and she replied that a prospective guide was introducing herself, "She wants to help you. She'll only stay if you accept her."

"My, she is tender. Every time she approaches, I feel so loved."

"Yes, she's an old soul who works closely with the light. You're very lucky to have her guidance. But now do your stuff and find out who she is. Clear your mind, and see what she has to tell you tonight."

First, I saw a splash of purple and it transformed to a soft violet with white and pink hues marbled through it. Slowly the collage became a flower and its petals reached to a white haze on the horizon of my mind. The vision disappeared. Next the back of a nun's veil appeared, and the figure turned sideways, revealing a thin white band around the forehead of a face I could not see.

"Now what do you see?" The instructor asked.

"She telling me that she was a nun, and I think the flower represents her nature. The colors are soft and beautiful." Then her face took form and I said, "She's beautiful . . . like an angel." My heart sped up as she drew near. "She's beautiful!"

"Yes, but there's more. So quiet your mind and let her introduce herself to you." Waves of love washed over me as I gazed at the nun. Then the screen went blank. Awed by her sweetness and beauty, I wanted to know more about her and what she had to say.

During the following weeks she revealed that her name was Therese and in her last life she was a French nun who lived around the turn of the century. She joined my band of spirits to teach me about love. Her simple approach to life as well as her loving disposition enamored me, and like a moth to a flame, I trusted her. Therese sent a flower and love before materializing in my mind. Weeks later she told me that some people referred to her as the Little Flower. She smiled and said, "Perhaps because I died so young in the convent."

One night I asked my instructor, "Was she a famous person in her last life?"

"Yes, she was. You are communicating well with her. I think you could find something written on her if you put your mind to it." She paused, squeezed her eyes shut and cocked her head as she communicated with her spirit guides. Then she said, "It's coming to me that she was French nun . . . yes . . . now I see the letter L. . . . That might be associated with a town . . . and she was a saint or something like that."

Therese, my spirit guide, divulged very little about her actual life on Earth, asserting that sharing her little way of truth and love was all that mattered. She said that the details of her life were inconsequential when compared to the magnificence of the spiritual reality. A model of modesty and sacrificial love, she regularly reiterated her desire to serve as my eyes and ears in a spiritual reality, inaccessible to me because of the limitations imposed by my physical body.

At the library I read about two Catholic saints named Therese, one of Avila and the other Lisieux. Shortly thereafter

I described my encounters with Sister Therese to my mother, a member of the Reorganized Church of the Latter-Day Saints. My mother also saw visions and communicated with angelic beings and souls residing in spirit. After our conversation she sent me Saint Therese's autobiography, *Story of a Soul.*

I read it while sitting in a lawn chair next to a pool where children splashed and dove for rocks thrown into the water. Oblivious to the ruckus, I soaked up the midsummer sun and devoured the story of Saint Therese of Lisieux, also known as the Little Flower. She was a French girl who became a Carmelite nun and suffered an agonizing death from tuberculosis at the age twenty-four in the late 1800s.[2]

The Therese in the story loved Jesus Christ, and I thought it curious my spirit guide never mentioned him to me. During a morning meditation I asked her about this, and she explained that upon entering the spirit world she discovered that there were many paths to God. She regretted putting one above the other.

I read that months before her death Sister Therese predicted that ". . . my heaven will be spent on earth . . . Yes, I want to spend my heaven in doing good on earth."[3] I thanked her for selecting me as a recipient of her "good on earth," to which she demurely replied, "I'm here to serve. It is my little way . . . the only way I know."

I believed that no one could feign a love as pure as hers, and my faith was further fueled by a visitation of my spirit guides to my husband in fall 1981. He described it this way.

---

2    *Story of a Soul: The Autobiography of Saint Therese of Lisieux, 3ʳᵈ ed.,* trans. by John Clarke O.C.D. (Washington DC: ICS Publications), 1.

3    Ibid., 263.

While deer hunting in the Colorado mountains, he was roused from a deep sleep by a knocking which he assumed came from someone at the door of his motel room. He started to get up but stopped when he saw with his naked eye a light expanding at the foot of his bed and three figures materialized. A soft glow emanated from the life-sized trio, consisting of a tall man flanked by two smaller women. He immediately recognized them as three spirit guides I had described. Sitting upright in the bed, he gazed at them and a peaceful feeling settled over him.

The woman attired in a nun's habit introduced herself as Sister Therese. The other female spirit guide said her name. Silence. My husband feared that their appearance meant that something dreadful had happened to me, and as if reading his thoughts, the male presence said, "Sharon is okay and so are you." Then silence. An incredible sense of peace pervaded the room and pushed away any apprehension he might have had at seeing the apparition. The spirits simply stared at him and he at them for an indeterminate period of time, and then they vanished. "I slept like a baby the rest of the night," he later told me, "They are incredible! What an amazing experience!"

His descriptions of the man's authoritative presence and Therese's beauty verified that my trust was well placed. The next week at my spiritual development class I asked the instructor if my guides would appear to me. I had only seen and heard them in my mind and wanted to see them fully formed. She said no and explained that they materialized to him in an effort to fortify his faith in the existence of the spirit world. Mine needed no such bolstering. Although slightly envious of his experience, I was glad they corroborated their existence. Seeing them face to face heightened his respect and belief in my spiritual pursuits. He witnessed firsthand what I knew to be true, namely, that these spirits could be trusted with the deepest parts of our life.

Having gained my trust, Sister Therese served as my guide during readings. For example, when practicing psychometry, a divination technique, I held a personal object belonging to the woman sitting next to me. The instructor said, "Personal objects emit vibrations, which tell us something about the person. As you give the reading, a spirit guide will assist you. They are here to support you as you develop in this area."

I clasped the woman's ring, closed my eyes, and cleared my mind. While holding the ring, a sweet, loving feeling came over me and I knew that Therese would assist me. In my mind's eye, I saw a swatch of black hair and then soft brown eyes and a brightly colored scarf. I opened my eyes and asked the woman if she knew someone who liked bright scarves and had dark brown eyes and black hair. Nodding, she said that her mother had had dark eyes and hair and liked bright scarves. Closing my eyes again, I sat quietly as Therese told me what to tell the woman. The information related to what she should do and how it would turn out. After I relayed the message, the woman tearfully said, "It's a relief to know that my mother is okay and aware of my struggle. I'll try to do what she suggested."

Next she meditated on my ring. As she gave my reading, I experienced sensations telling me whether to reject or accept what she said. My intuition, scenes in my mind, and feelings of elation punctuated what was said. The reading would have sounded inane to objective observers, but they could not see, feel, or hear how demons embellished it inside me. In fact, the inspiration proffered by demons during the reading more confirmed the spiritual source than whether the prediction came true. Furthermore, the inspiration targeted areas of utmost concern, such as, relationships, personal functioning, and spiritual growth. This confirmed that the spirits understood my plight and helped as I deemed necessary.

During the years I practiced as a psychic, many people assessed me to be the "real thing." Using the criteria of conventional wisdom, they evaluated my performance and character. Indeed, I was sincere, interested in people, positive, able to relay information about which I had no prior knowledge, gave pertinent counsel, and spoke philosophically about their lives. Sometimes the predictions came true and sometimes not, but I counseled that one could not expect one hundred percent accuracy. I thought we lived in an unfolding universe, meaning that the future consisted of probabilities rather than definite outcomes. Mostly my counsel related to personal situations and how decisions affected spiritual growth. Finally in 1984, seven years after joining the class, my guides spoke through me. I sat erect but comfortably in a folding chair, breathed deeply, and cleared my mind. As a thought came, I gave it no energy and instead looked at the black expanse in my mind's eye. I further released my spirit and entered the twilight place experienced between sleep and wakefulness, fully present but disengaged. I waited for guidance.

I drifted further away, and as I did, another presence swished into my body, moved my mouth, blinked my eyes, and exercised the muscles of my face. He talked. I listened from my distant shelf, fully confident I could exercise my right to reenter my body if I chose. But I saw no need. In a respectful manner, he related positive, uplifting, and personally encouraging messages. When the reading ended, he exited as quickly as he came, and I became fully myself and present to the person seated across from me.

The spirits came only when invited and left when the session concluded. I never questioned their intentions or character—that is, until January 1985, when the one called Seth turned on me after I refused to communicate material that I thought would frighten people and told them I no longer wanted to be a medium.

I sat on the step outside my house and watched the brown cassette ribbon flap in the wind. Clasping my hands together, I prayed, "Oh God, help me. There has to be more to this spiritual universe than evil appearing good. Where can I go? Where can I turn? Who can save me from this evil? Help me, O God, I beg you, help me." The sun warmed me, but a biting wind cut to the bone as I stood to go inside, glanced mechanically at the blue sky, and resolved to call a friend.

# CHAPTER 6

# My Search for Wisdom

*But where can wisdom be found? Where does understanding dwell?* (Job 28:12).

*I had embraced secular humanism which offered no defense against spiritual evil.*

### March 1986

TALL, BARE TREES BORDERED THE trail and framed the gray sky. Patches of green pushed through clumps of snow, and tiny yellow flowers played peek-a-boo, contributing color to an otherwise bland landscape. I thought about the passing seasons and searched for signs of spring as my friend and I walked along. Winter gave way to spring, spring to summer—everything changed into something else. It had to! All of creation must respond to something greater than itself and to the natural order of life. I fixed my gaze on the tiny yellow messengers as we walked down the path.

The spring snow had melted quickly and muddied our walking path, so Joan and I played hopscotch around the muck on our Sunday morning walk. "Does this path resemble our lives or what?" she joked. A practicing psychotherapist and friend for several years, she also had taken a circuitous spiritual journey, but she had left her group when it "got too weird." Although she never channeled, she explored the spirit-mind-body relationship and believed in spirits and in evil. Now she wrestled with mundane problems like the absence of men and money in her life.

I listened and walked alongside as she spun the details of her life. I had no difficulty understanding her problems, but would she understand mine? Even with her experience, I doubted she could fathom the horror of my inner life, so I decided to paint my life in broad strokes and judge from her response if I should say more.

Joan concluded her tale and waited for me to talk about myself. My mind froze as if wedged in a vice. Nothing flowed in or out. I can't do this, I thought. It's too bizarre!

She turned and asked, "What have you been doing? Seems like a long time since we've talked. Are you all right?"

"No. I'm not."

"What's wrong?"

Now the door was open, and I responded, "I'm in deep trouble spiritually, and I don't know what to do."

"What happened?"

"Well, you know those spirits I channeled?"

Joan's face registered her concern as she replied, "Yes, I remember. Last I heard, you were conducting your practice and channeling in the classes. What changed?"

"Well, a year ago, I noticed that my life wasn't going very well. The spirits were asking for more of my time and attention, and I was beginning to feel as if my life were not my own. About that time, the spirits asked me to predict that a nuclear holocaust would devastate the planet in the summer of 1987. At first I wrote their discourse because they had never given me a reason to mistrust them, but the message frightened me, and I knew it would frighten others.

Finally, I told them that I didn't want to convey the message and that I intended to stop channeling. I really wanted to do more of my own thinking. They seemed disappointed but wished me well. The next morning, I awoke consumed by an evil presence. It was an odious spirit—raw and vile—like something I thought existed only in the movies. I begged him to leave, but my pleading seemed to make matters worse. Because he was so hard to cope with, I closed my practice and simply endured his torture. Then last September he let up and I started to work again. My other guides tried to help as best they could.

Then last week, during breakfast, every one of them attacked me . . . after all those years of helping and acting so loving, they suddenly turned on me. They had fooled me with their charade of caring and compassion. Liars—every one of them evil—now control my body and mind. I don't know how to make them leave!"

More than anything I wanted my friend to understand, but I talked without emotion—like a reporter recounting someone else's life. How could she know that I no longer expressed emotions spontaneously? To survive, I passed all experiences through my grid of what I thought appropriate. What grid did she use? How was she organizing my words in her head? I continued in a matter-of-fact tone.

"The spirits bombard me with accusations and disgusting feelings. And all I know to do is to live as if they are not there and accept thoughts or feelings if they reflect the person I remember myself to be. Mostly I ignore my inner life." Feeling embarrassed and overexposed, I added, "It is so bizarre! I can't believe I'm saying these things to you!"

Spirit voices grew louder in my mind and jeered, "Whiner! Little medium getting all beat up and gonna cry on her shoulder? No use; we control what happens here! We've told her we can only influence evil people and those who channel spirits. She has nothing to worry about. You're the stupid one!" As they threatened and accused, I willfully directed my attention to my friend and the yellow flowers along the path.

"That sounds terrible! I'm sure it's easier to be with friends than alone." Then she said, "Yes, I believe evil exists. When I hear of men raping women or mutilating children, I know that psychotherapy can't help them. It's beyond a personality problem. They're just evil."

"Yes," I responded, "I think psychology has overstepped its bounds by assuming that it can help everyone. I know I'm not mentally ill as it's usually defined, but the presence of these spirits has taken its toll on me." I shuddered at the prospect of what this diabolical force could do to people with a limited understanding of themselves or their emotions, or who had poor impulse control or a fragile hold on reality.

The summer before, I had stood next to a lady as she paid for a soft drink at a food court in a large mall. As if in slow motion and hampered by a tremor in her hands, she struggled to count her pennies, nickels, and quarters as people shifted impatiently behind her. Tall, thin, and disheveled, she held her ragged purse under her left arm, carefully fingered the coins one at a time, and placed them on the counter. She ignored a penny as it rolled across the counter, teetered on the edge, and fell to the floor. Her yellow-stained fingers picked and delivered the $1.25 to the cashier. But her dull eyes scarcely acknowledged the accomplishment, and with soft drink in hand, she shuffled to a table. Through it all, the woman's lips conversed with an unseen someone, and I could only imagine the torment that consumed her. The simplest task required everything she had, and I wanted to hold her and say, "I know what it's like, and it's not all you. You are a person worth fighting for. Don't give up. Resist their lies." During my twenties, I had worked at a state mental hospital and witnessed others who struggled with voices. Some were schizophrenic as this woman appeared to be. I knew the disease had a genetic and biochemical component but wondered if in addition she battled the same evil in her mind as I did. Her vulnerability to spiritual torment moved me to tears.

I wondered to what extent this evil invaded the lives of others and influenced their thinking and behaving. I wanted to explore this with my friend but knew that in my present condition I was incapable of such a discussion. First I had to get free.

I turned to Joan and said, "I honestly don't know where to turn. I have thought of therapy, but I'm afraid they'll hear the symptoms and assume psychosis. The thought of taking an anti-psychotic medication terrifies me. I'm afraid I'd lose all ability to discern myself from the spirits. You know most therapists simply don't believe in evil spirits or their ability to systematically destroy a person. To them, evil is a concept or metaphor for the darker side of a personality."

She laughed ruefully and said, "No. I think it best that you avoid seeking help from a therapist."

"I did think of going to a Jungian therapist. But Jung talked with a spirit, and it makes me wonder how much it influenced him as he developed his theories." I added, "I will never accept that these tormentors are part of me!"

"Who else can help?"

"Last week I called a pastor at a Unity church I occasionally attend. Their service is lovely . . . somewhat Christian in that they pray, sing the Lord's Prayer, and have a sermon. But they believe there are many paths to God. They sponsor study groups for the *Course in Miracles*. Have you heard of that?"

Joan nodded, "Yes. The books were channeled by a spirit called Jesus."

"Yes, and that's a good reason not to trust it. But I thought if anyone would understand my situation, it would be this pastor. He cut me off short and told me to go elsewhere. And when I asked where, he said, 'I don't know' and hung up."

My story fueled Joan's deep mistrust of organized religion, and she said, "Can you believe that a pastor would turn you away? Hypocrites! That's why I don't go near those buildings."

"I also contacted the minister at the spiritualist church, and he basically treated me the same way saying that I should have known to stay focused on the light. He said that I had somehow attracted this evil into my life. 'How?' I asked. And he emphatically reiterated that I opened a door, invited evil in, and only I could close it. And that was it! Conversation over. Can you believe that?"

"No, I can't."

"I'll do anything to get free." I stopped and turned to her, "But the answer has to be of a spiritual nature. Don't you think?"

She nodded, and we continued our trek in silence, "A friend of mine meditates with devotees of Sai Baba. They don't channel," she reassured, "and perhaps she could help you. Sai Baba is a powerful healer from India."

"Yes, I'm willing to try."

I breathed deeply the scents of spring and lifted my face toward the warmth of the midmorning sun. Spring symbolized beginnings, and surely my time had come. Our path a little drier,

Joan and I walked with less trepidation as we neared our cars. We hugged and arranged to meet the next Sunday morning.

Sharing the burden of my life lightened my load, and as I drove home, I felt a tinge of optimism. I clung to the hope that new life lived in my spirit, and like the buds on the bare trees, I too would bud and blossom again. Just as grass pushed through the snow, flowers burst out of pods, and the sun warmed the earth, the natural order of life would provide a way of escape and sustenance for me. The world of spirit responded to the same laws as nature. Did it not? Otherwise evil and chaos would prevail on Earth, and our best efforts would be in vain. No, surely even these spirits must respond to something greater. Yet what must I do to resolve this conflict? What role did I play? How does one fight a force that manipulates mind and emotions from the inside out? I thought that by developing a strong identity, pursuing good, taking responsibility for myself, and helping others, I could circumvent this battle. I learned through the Human Potential Movement that entered American culture in the late 1960s.

### Spring 1966

If not for the attention she received, I would not have known she was Virginia Satir, a reputed leader in the Human Potential Movement and one of the founders of the Esalen Institute in California. She dressed in beige, loose fitting slacks; a pale, print blouse, and walking shoes, and she wore her authority as casually as her clothes. I heard her say, "Then what happened? And then did you . . . ?" She was leading a twenty-four-hour marathon sponsored by the hospital where I worked.

She laughed, her question deftly pointing to the heart of the matter. She pushed past the surface as if unafraid of what might lurk beneath the words. I had never met anyone quite like her. I watched her touch people's lives in ways that went beneath the surface to what really mattered. She exuded power, but a kind I had not encountered before, for it seemed to emanate from a fearless place, one in which vulnerability, strength, and caring comfortably coexisted.

As Virginia closed the workshop, she said, "Together we faced the hurtful places, released the pain, and learned to love— really love. You are good people who have failed to thrive for lack of nourishment. Allow yourself to believe this and create relationships that foster growth and love. You came into this world beautiful—now become it! And help others to do likewise!"

I accepted the challenge. For the next ten years I examined events and relationships in my upbringing that fostered low self-esteem and an inability to believe in myself. I discarded thoughts and feelings reflective of a low opinion of myself, such as guilt and self-doubt, and learned to trust my feelings, intuitions, and my ability to overcome obstacles and succeed. Through the years, I conducted personal growth groups, established a private practice in marriage and family therapy, and trained others in the techniques and philosophy of experiential therapies like the work of Virginia Satir. Human secularism supplanted my Christian faith and later blended well with New Age thought.

Yet, the interplay between human responsibility, mental illness, and spiritual interference confounded me.

### 1950

I had watched my mother struggle against unseen forces. Like a reed swaying whichever way the wind sent her, she seemed to vacate herself and succumb to forces more powerful than herself. I vowed never to let that happen to me.

My dad had told my mother, "Never let those Watchtower ladies in this house!" He was often away on business, however, and again that afternoon my mother let them in. They huddled on the couch fingering their thin pamphlet and conferring in urgent, hushed tones. Mother fervently paged the Bible as if with their help she could at last solve the great mysteries of God—mysteries not dealt with at the Presbyterian Church. The women leaned closer, took my mother's hands in theirs, and prayed. Their arms encircled her shoulders as she pleaded with God to show himself to her.

That night as we sat in an overstuffed chair listening to the radio, I combed her hair, and although I was only eight years old, I sensed that a crack went deep into my mother's soul. As if applying salve to a severed limb, I stroked her hair and petted her face, and as each tangle gave way to the pull of my brush, the weary lines loosened on her face. Though strong feelings generally embarrassed her, that night my mother accepted tenderness.

A couple days later my mother paraded regally through the house dressed in a purple robe. She stood poised halfway up the stairs and stared hard at me with cold, haughty eyes and said, "God proclaims I am the Virgin Mary . . . set apart from others. I now go to my room, and no one enters without my permission." She turned and slowly ascended the stairs. Slam! Her bedroom door closed.

Talking to Jesus I understood, and my mother's name was Mary, but I knew she could only pretend to be the Virgin Mary, not really be her! Not knowing what else to do, I sat outside her door until my fourteen-year-old sister came home.

Within a couple days my father admitted my mother to a sanitarium. He said that the strain of raising four children had been too much for her. We visited a month later. Dimly aware of the adult discussions, I looked through the barred window into the bare tiled room of the sanitarium. A solitary woman frantically paced back and forth rubbing her hands together. Her cotton dress hung loosely to her ankles, and her tangled hair stood on end. Suddenly she stopped, locked her arms around herself, and rocked from heel to toe, all the while muttering to the unseen. Then she whirled to stare hard at me. I stifled a cry as I recognized my mother. She did not know me. With bars and the width of the room between us, I gaped as my mother resumed her pacing, then held herself and rocked, all the while talking with an unseen someone. Oh, her pain!

"Come back! You're my mom. Come back!" I silently screamed. I turned to search my father's face. Visibly shaken, he uttered, "The shock treatments—it's because of the shock treatments. It's temporary. She will be herself again; the doctors said so." Covering my terror with a smile, I took his hand. I lost faith in my mother that day. I stepped back and no longer trusted her to help me find my way.

Dazed by a hundred or more shock treatments, my mother returned home with little memory of my childhood. Intellectually impaired, emotionally fragile, and spiritually depleted, she retreated to music for solace and repair. She spent hours singing operas and playing her favorite classics.

My family lacked the skills and understanding to discuss my mother's condition, and so we overlooked her difficulties, treated her kindly, and waited for her memory to return. Most of it did, and step-by-step she became herself again.

My mother's last psychotic break occurred during my freshman year in college. My father died two years later, February 1963, and soon after, my mother left the Presbyterian Church to join the "real church of Joseph Smith." When I called it Mormon, she corrected me and told me it was the Reorganized Church of the Latter-Day Saints, whose headquarters were in Independence, Missouri. Eventually she moved there. I thought Mormons were an ultraconservative Christian denomination and that at last she had found a spiritual home among people who applauded her communications with spirits and her efforts to be like God. She remained with them until her death in September 1985.

I dedicated my life to not replicating hers and yet suspected that the same enemy that vexed her now tormented me. Was it an accident that the spirits took control of me the year she died? I could not say. And yet I knew she died still their prisoner, and I reckoned the Christian church would be of no help to me either. But what part could I play in securing my freedom?

As I drove home, I glanced at the lime-colored branches stretched against the blue sky and uttered encouraging words to myself, "If I do my part, the universe will provide. New life will grow in me. But nothing will happen unless I seek it. I'm part of nature and must do my part to get back into the stream of life. Somewhere, somehow I'll find the answer." I sighed, breathing deeply, "Where should I step next?"

# CHAPTER 7

# The Day I Rejected God

*But you have now rejected your God, who saves you out of all your disasters and calamities.* (1 Sam. 10:19).

*A string of family tragedies weakened my childhood faith in God. I rebelled and turned from Holy God. I rejected the only One who could save me.*

I HAD A CLOSE RELATIONSHIP with Jesus as a child, but my faith was shaken after my father suffered a heart attack when I was ten. The doctor warned that unless my father lost a hundred pounds, he would die. We all pitched in to help him live. We boiled eggs and broiled meat. We walked alongside as he bought groceries, serviced his car, and attended church. We were always available in case he cried for help and needed us to call an ambulance.

A couple months after the attack, I smiled between a spoonful of Campbell's tomato soup at my father who came to the kitchen table. "Want me to put the water on?" I offered.

"Yes, sounds good!" He ate two soft-boiled eggs on two pieces of dry toast twice a day.

"No fried, greasy foods for this man," he boasted and, shifting his eyes, whispered, "but could you top that egg with some creamy fudge?" He laughed.

Dad put on a serious face as he sat. He sighed deeply, "Something wonderful happened to me." A quiver entered his voice, and I pushed my soup bowl aside and stared at my father. He continued, "I prayed that Jesus Christ would help me, and suddenly his Spirit filled me up!" He shyly said, "They call it being 'titched by the Holy Ghost.'" His eyes glistened as he continued. "I rededicated my life to Jesus Christ, and God filled me with joy like I've never known." Love seemed to radiate from him, and I sensed that he had the same love for Jesus that I carried in my heart. I left my chair to wrap my arms around his neck.

"I'm happy for you, Dad. I love you very much."

He wiped the wetness from his eyes as we silently shared our hug. "Your mother and I have decided to pray and read the Bible together as a family every night before going to sleep."

It was during a family devotional hour a month later that my father announced another change in our family. "Your mother and I have decided that because of my heart condition, she must travel with me on the road." My dad had that "please understand and make the best of it" look as his eyes moved from one child to the next. "I must support this family, and if something should happen to me, your mother would be available to call the doctor." Though he didn't say it outright, his meaning was clear to me: "I don't want to die alone, and maybe your mother will save my life."

"We will be gone for two or three weeks at a time and home for a weekend. We'll call every night to make sure you're okay. Your sister will be in charge while we're gone. I'm counting on you to obey her."

We all nodded—my eighteen-year-old sister, eight- and five-year-old brothers, and I. "Of course, I would do my part," I thought. "It must be terrible to be that afraid of dying."

Soon after and for the next three years they left Monday morning and returned two or three weeks later just in time for supper and left the following Monday. When I was a junior in high school, they came home every weekend. My sister left home during the first year, and they hired housekeepers to care for my brothers and me. After several housekeepers left, they brought my great-aunt from Independence, Missouri, to live with us.

At first the knowledge that my father loved me offered solace and hope, much like a bright star in the heavens, but by the time I was thirteen, I realized that he knew nothing of the actual terrain of my life. As my parents' goings and comings became a fixed pattern, I retreated emotionally from both of them, thinking of them less and less each day.

One afternoon I waited for my parents to come home. The white organza curtains draped to the side allowing me a bird's-eye view of the street below as I sat on the foot of my bed. Generally, my father leaned on his horn while yet a block down the tree-lined street, signaling my brothers and me to drop everything, rush to the curb, and greet them as they pulled into the driveway. I dreaded the sound. "Why?" I asked myself. "My folks are coming home. I should be happy." But I wasn't. There was always too much to say in too little time, and I usually thought of the really important things after they left. Mostly it was easier to pretend I had no parents—that is, until I heard the horn. The horn blared, and I reflexively leaped from the bed, raced to the curbside, waved my arms, and smiled broadly as they turned in the driveway. But I no longer beamed from my heart. Did they notice? I don't think so.

During my early teen years, I lost faith in my father, let go of his hand. Though I continued to love him, I hated his dependency on my mother as well as his fear of dying, and I vowed that neither fear or dependency would ever control me. When he was home, we laughed and played. But we both knew I had to manage my life without him.

My faith remained strong as I sat in an auditorium filled with seventh-, eighth-, and ninth-graders as the teacher stood at the podium shuffling papers containing the names of the new cheerleaders. Sweat trickled down my side and my heart pounded as I instinctively covered my face with clammy hands and prayed, "I want it so bad, but oh, Lord Jesus, please help me love the girl who gets it. Please, Lord, don't let me resent her!" When I heard her name called, my heart miraculously leaped with joy Tears of gratitude filled my eyes, and I prayed, "Thank you, Lord Jesus. Thank you." Rejoicing as if the winner, I wove through the screaming swarm and threw my arms around her.

It never occurred to me to pray for myself. In fact, I thought that was selfish. More than anything I wanted to please Jesus, and to do so I thought I must deny myself and love others. Often I interpreted that to mean that God disapproved if I wanted something for myself, and this was especially true if someone seemed more in need than me. Under those circumstances, I had no rights. Therefore, I never talked to God about my loneliness or how unprotected I felt with my parents gone. I only approached him when I sensed I was not measuring up to his expectations. Yet when I did, he always brought me great joy. I associated this feeling with pleasing him and continued discounting my needs and feelings.

This stance of mine proved most difficult when, shortly before my fifteenth birthday, I fell in love with a boy, and he loved me. His father, a minister, was called to a church out of state. I opened my heart very wide, and when he left, it would not close. Gone was the love and sense of wonder, and all that was left was an emptiness that dipped into a dark, deep hole. Still, I never talked to Jesus about it. In the same way that my mother and father said they loved me but left, I believed that God loved me and expected me to love others—regardless.

I faithfully attended church, and while seated one Sunday, a commotion in the back jarred me from my reverie. I turned and glimpsed ten slovenly dressed men and women. I heard, "Gypsies!" They reached the minister with outstretched arms and begged, "Please baptize our children. Baptize. Please." He raised his eyes from his notes only briefly before shooing them away with a slight movement of his wrist. Then he raised his voice, so parishioners could hear the sermon above the commotion caused by the motley group as the ushers shepherded them out the door.

Mentally I screamed, "Hypocrites! What about 'when you do this to the least of these, you do it to me'? What about that Scripture? Or does that only apply to the rest of us, Pastor?"

Consumed by rage, I continued the attack. "You ignore it. My parents ignore it. Maybe I'm the fool for taking it so seriously. Is Jesus who you say he is, or this a game of pretend? Is it? And what about the Bible? Are we to follow it or not? What's real here anyway?"

I glared at the pastor, and my heart hardened. "I'll decide for myself what to believe and no longer look to any of you. You're not who you say you are." I gathered my belongings and, smiling appropriately, left without saying a word.

"I'll take care of myself," I vowed as I walked home. "What they ask is impossible! They want me to be a perfect person, yet they offer absolutely no help. Then they do as they please. Well, no more. I quit!" In my heart I deemed all authority as irrelevant to my daily existence and concluded that only children actually believed the Bible. It was time to grow up and join the world.

I did: school, success, parties, laughter, gossip, sports, dating, projects, boyfriends, awards, honors, moving fast, never home, going, running. At age sixteen I glided toward the end of the three-meter diving board, brought my right foot down hard, and sprang upward. My body soared like a bird till I reached the peak of the ascent. Then I lifted my legs to meet my hands, jackknifed—suspended. Released. My head pulled toward the water, and my body straightened for the entry. Splash—I plunged to the bottom of the pool like a projective freed from its casing. Freedom. That's what I asked for.

My father died when I was twenty, ten years after his first heart attack. My mother heard his cry from the next room, "Mary. Mary." She ran and held him as he released his last breath. "He died so peacefully, so free from fear," she said when I arrived home from college early the next morning. "Yesterday he came to me with his Bible and asked me to read and pray with him. We did so all afternoon."

I closed my eyes and bowed my head to cover my ache. I whispered, "Father, must you leave completely? It's too soon to be on my own. I still need a dad, someone, somewhere to protect me a while longer. Of course, I can make it alone, but it's so hard, Daddy. Did you know? Did you know how hard it was all those years with the two of you gone? So hard."

# CHAPTER 8

# I Turned to False Gods

*How long will you people turn my glory into shame? How long will you love delusions and seek false gods?* (Psalm 4:2).

*The Enemy of God inspired powerful spiritual experiences that enlivened me. But the phenomena inevitably dissipated. It never produced substantive change—only bondage. Like-minded friends tried to help me.*

### Spring 1986

MOLLY'S GENTLE FACE HOVERED A couple inches above mine as she cradled the back of my neck with her right hand and lightly touched the center of my forehead with her left index and middle fingers. Smells of rose water and incense washed my senses, and my stomach gurgled from the warm chamomile tea peppered with lemon. "See? You're already opening!" Responding to the rumblings of my stomach, she exclaimed, "Soon the blockages will clear. I'll hold the pressure points along the center meridian, releasing the life force along your chakras. Then I'll check your pulses. I'm afraid you're depleted down to the core of you! I'm so glad you called. It's great to see you again."

Her hands lovingly massaged my "third eye" until she felt a pulsation in her fingertips. Then, after mentally deliberating with her spirit guides, she moved her fingers to another pressure point. My chest rose and fell, filling with and releasing the precious breath of life, and with each exhalation and inhalation, I sank deeper into the white sheet covering her Jin Shin Juytsu treatment table.

I believed that as she touched me she transmitted energy from her spirit to mine. Much as a jumper cable transfers electrical energy from a fully functioning car to one stalled, her hands served as a conduit from her spirit to mine. Our spirits were linked to God, and once she released the blockages, my spiritual energies would flow through my beleaguered body and heal it.

I lay still and for an instant felt swathed in a blanket of love, satiated and fully protected from evil. I recalled the promises of spirit: "Let go! Open your heart and mind. Remove barriers that disallow your spirit merging with those of a like nature. Confront your fears, those false illusions appearing real." I cringed.

Molly deftly moved from one point to another for an hour and then lifted my wrists to check my pulse. She lowered her head, closed her eyes, and appeared to go deeply within herself. Then as if straining to capture Wisdom itself, she wrinkled her forehead and held her pensive position. A sweet smile signaled her success, and gently stroking my arm, she said, "That is all we can do today, but perhaps within a couple days we can meet again. I trust your karma will be resolved soon and you'll look back and understand completely the purpose of this torment. Take heart; I love you so much, and it pains me to see you suffer."

A gentle woman in her mid-thirties, Molly had dedicated her life to helping others heal. She opened her hands, arms, and heart to those who stumbled on their spiritual paths. She believed, as

I did, that we were responsible for confronting the disease in our lives.

"I made a serious error somewhere along the way, but I don't know how or where. Your spirits haven't turned on you, so why have mine on me? Perhaps it's because I channeled. Could that have been my mistake? I've relied on myself since I was a girl and never have I been so totally incapable of directing my life."

Molly shook her head in wonderment at the mysteries of the universe. "Imagine, Sharon, the yin and yang forces of universal life destroying and then creating life as we know it in the spiritual and physical universe. We play our part in this universal drama, and for important reasons, you are going through a period of destruction, but wait . . . wait! Your time will come. The rebuilding is so much fun!" She wrapped her arms around me, held me tight, and whispered, "Your time will come."

I hugged her back but shook my head and admitted, "I no longer know what to believe. It's like an icy abyss has replaced my heart, and my mind is incapable of an original thought. Love seems more like a concept than reality, and I function by remembering how I used to act. These evil spirits have ravaged me, Molly."

I could talk to her in this way, for I knew that her open arms and compassionate gaze camouflaged a trembling, tender heart badly in need of repair. She too sought a refuge for her gentle spirit, but like an enchanted butterfly sipping nectar from succulent flowers, she satiated her hungers by flitting from one experience to another.

"Oh, Molly, I won't give up, but I'm tired of doing this alone. So tired."

She took my hand in hers and smiled. "I'm here for you. Call me."

Then I met with the Sai Baba Group.

A wide candle sat on the pale cloth covering the makeshift if altar, and its flickering flame served as a point of focus for our meditation. Discordant strains filtering from beneath the table and pulsating in sync with winking shadows in the sparsely furnished room cast an other-worldly mood throughout the inner-city duplex where six devotees gathered to pay homage to Sai Baba.

First the breath—a steady inhaling of the life force, an imperceptible pause, and gentle release back to the universe. What began as conscious labor now transformed to seamless flow, requiring mere observation on my part, no engagement of my will. I took in and emptied, filled up and let go, and as I did, I enacted a process endemic to all life.

Buddhists, Hindus, aborigines, even astrologers, transcendentalists, and psychologists—they all described the cycles of birth/death, day/night, wake/sleep, young/old, summer/winter, yin/yang as timeless reflections of a process intrinsic to personal development as well as to the unfolding universe.

In the summer of 1982, I had studied the aboriginal worldview with an American white man who as a teenager had made a pilgrimage to India to live on an ashram and learn from a holy man. He returned to the United States in his twenties armed with a new name and philosophy, and he found a spiritual mentor, a shaman and member of an Indian tribe located in a remote area of Mexico. While living there, he married a member of the tribe and adopted their aboriginal beliefs and customs and became a shaman. He looked to be in his thirties when conducting his workshop at Esalen. The institute was hailed as a bastion of the human potential movement and on the cutting edge of alternative spiritual expressions, and his seminar on the medicine wheel had received acclaim for its authentic approach to Native American spirituality.

Through this shaman and later a doctoral advisor, I discovered that other religions relied on the mandala as well, for it aptly depicted life as a never-ending series of happenings in which present circumstances set the stage for future ones. What I learned in my studies of the medicine wheel and later with Lakota Sioux shamans helped me grasp the basic assumptions of the Tao, Hinduism, and Buddhism.

Before daybreak the men dug a pit a short distance from where the ocean spit its foam while crashing against the jagged boulders on the California coast. The pit was sandwiched between the Pacific and an embankment that jutted about thirty feet upward to cliffs looming overhead.

The sweat lodge itself was shaped like an igloo and consisted of limber branches bent and bound to form the skeleton of a hutch that was covered with animal skins to darken the interior. It reminded me of half a coconut turned upside down, but I dared not tease, for I had been told that the preparatory activities were sacred and directed by "Spirit," the shamans' term for God. This shaman had already made a concession by allowing women to participate, and then only if they were not menstruating, which was considered unclean. I feared that if I made light of any part of the ceremony, he would ban me from participating.

In addition to building the lodge, we prepared by fasting and drumming and by building and stoking the fire. When the embers glowed, we dumped eight or so cushion-sized rocks into flames that blazed upward ten feet into the air. Later the piping-hot rocks would be retrieved with a pitch fork and be shoveled into the pit at the center of the sweat lodge. When doused with water, the steam permeated the lodge and every pore on our bodies, pushing our temperatures well above normal-ideal for a purification ceremony.

Preparing for the ceremony took most of the day, while the actual event lasted only a little over an hour. We expected to finish by four o'clock in the afternoon, at which time we would break our fast with fruit and lots of water. At about eleven o'clock our leader directed us to meditate on Mother Earth. He assured that as we did, our spirit would merge with a primordial consciousness within the Earth and awaken a like energy within us. He said, "Meditate on the Earth. Allow your spirit to become one with it. Let a stone speak to you, and then pick it up. Meditate on it. At the right time—you'll know when—bring it back to the fire."

Like other shamans, he believed the Earth spirit spoke to him—not outright, but through visions, sensations, and his spirit. He previously warned that communicating with spirits that appeared in human form was taboo, for they were of a lower nature. But when we saw a totem—that is, a spirit materializing or taking the form of an animal—we should heed its counsel.

We dutifully meditated, retrieved our rocks, and gathered around the fire. The shaman's helper, Tom, beat a water drum he had tied that morning. He had filled an iron pot about a foot in diameter with water until it was three-quarters full and then stretched a piece of leather over the top. He secured it by tying a cord end over end, using a method divined by the shamans. When properly stretched and tied, he beat it with a wooden stick.

The sound reverberated through the water and seemed to penetrate to my marrow. The night before, the two of them had beat the drum for eight hours straight, relieving the other when one was tired. They broke rhythm to drench the leather when the tone grew hollow. They wetted the drum by tipping it until water pooled on top, then righted it and resumed their steady beat as we meditated.

Tom pounded slowly and at other times fast, but he always concentrated on the spot producing the deepest tone, which he said, "merged our souls with the pulsations of Mother Earth." Tom's reverent demeanor and the shaman's reiterations, "Drumming is sacred," convinced me that we were paying homage to the primordial girding for life itself. We worshiped, honoring Mother Earth as the giver and sustainer of life.

Tom beat the drum as we twelve sat around the fire learning about the medicine wheel, "The sweat lodge is a circle like the medicine wheel. We enter the lodge for purification. This is the medicine way." I thought, "Purification, first through the fast and now the heat. Release, Sharon; reach for yet another level of understanding of your place in the spiritual universe." I proudly accepted his challenge to abandon myself to the medicine way. "The four directions further tell the story, and once in the lodge we sit in the east, south, west, and north. Remember the medicine wheel is life. The sun rises in the east, the beginning; life explodes into action in the south; the setting sun signals a retreat inward; and ice crystals form in the north as wisdom is distilled from experience." His voice fell in step with the beat of the drum, and I felt transported to another realm.

"Travel the medicine wheel, the circle of life. In the east they see visions. Yet visions are worthless without the reflections of the west; and wisdom cuts without the heart of the south. We release our spirit to Father Sun, Mother Earth, to fire, wind, water, air."

The whitecaps slammed the rocks, spewing a fine mist into the air, and rays of sunlight filtered through tiny droplets, casting an iridescent haze overhead. But nature's prism transformed to a shimmering cloak of hot air as it neared our fire, and I marveled at the majesty and mystery of nature. Spirit resides in all of life, I thought reverently. Who could deny its power!

"Your spirit will lead you to your place in the circle," he encouraged. We removed our outer clothes, and clothed in bathing suits, we stooped to step through the four-by-three-foot opening and into the sweat lodge.

Instinctively, I sat in the east. Tom shoveled four rocks into the pit and took his place in the west. The drum resounded, and the shaman poured cups of water, followed by strings of sage, over the red-hot stones. He then swept the smoke with his long eagle feather to cleanse the lodge of unwanted spirits. He beat the drum slowly and chanted a penetrating wail. Wafts of burning sage bathed my senses as I sat cross-legged, clutching my gray, washed-smooth stone. I closed my eyes and began meditation by concentrating on inhaling and releasing my breath but quickly shifted to the pulse of the drum.

Fifteen minutes into the ceremony, an elderly man, looking deathly white, gently put his face to the ground, muttering that he felt faint but that we need not worry about him. No one did, and thirty minutes later he sat up. Every fifteen minutes the door flap opened and stones, fresh from the fire, replaced the cooled stones. This was followed by more water, heat, drumming, words, and visions. It reached a frenzied pitch and then subsided.

I presented a vibrant array of visions, and together we produced a symphony of experiences. I developed a splitting headache accompanied by nausea during the last fifteen minutes, probably due to dehydration, although some held a more spiritual interpretation. They insisted my body expelled toxins.

Years of meditating had prepared me well for the sweat lodge. I could attain an altered state of consciousness within seconds. I transcended the physical realm effortlessly, leaving behind my worldly perspective to reach for higher levels of understanding. I thought here I would know the truth of my situation and ascertain right thought and action. I worked to improve the conditions within and around me—to love more deeply, experience peace, feel whole, and live in harmony with my environment.

So much of what I had read and heard supported this worldview, and now four years later I sat with spiritual sojourners of a different sort. No sweat drenched my body or mournful cries assailed my ears, but here high-pitched songs in minor keys and quiet meditations soothed me, helped me transcend.

"Lord Sayta Sai Baba," the worshipers chanted, "Lord Krishna, Lord Jesus." The devotees praised the avatars, the incarnations of the godhead, and especially bowed low to Sai Baba, who reportedly produced precious stones from the air, miraculously healed blindness, drove out evil spirits, and relieved physical suffering. People converged at his ashram, situated near the village of Puttapati, India, to glimpse his person or touch him.

My chest barely stirred during this phase of my meditation, similar to those moments preceding sleep. I was neither awake nor asleep, but suspended between two realities, yet my mind remained fully alert. As if an audience, I listened to the tormentors in my mind, the music, and the devotees professing love for Sai Baba-suspended and waiting. Waiting for what? Him to free me? How? How does this work?

"Is Sai Baba who he says he is?" I asked myself. "I sing the songs and do what they say, but shouldn't he help me in some way?" After three months of meditating weekly, I noted that nothing had changed.

"Lord Sayta Sai Baba, Lord Jesus," they sang.

Lord Jesus . . . Lord . . . Why call him Lord? I thought as the devotees praised the avatars.

"Lord Sayta Sai Baba," they chanted. I sang along, but it meant nothing to me, and I grew weary of the pretense. I hated to leave these gentle people. I would like to have believed, for I desperately needed kindness in my life, but I sensed that 'Sai Baba was not who he said he was. Being able to manipulate the supernatural mattered little to me. I put no stock in someone's ability to produce miracles or see visions; those experiences were commonplace in my world. No, I sought a spiritual presence who was who he professed to be, and I desired to be with people who truly loved one another. I only hoped that my idealism would not again play me the fool.

I thanked them and left. I had nowhere else to turn.

# CHAPTER 9

# I Saw Evidence of God in Creation

*For since the creation of the world God's invisible qualities—his eternal power and divine nature—have been clearly seen, being understood from what has been made, so that people are without excuse* (Rom. 1:20).

*The beauty and stability of God's world convinced me that evil did not have ultimate authority. It did not point me to Jesus, but it gave me hope that one day I would be saved.*

SOON AFTER THE DEMONS TOOK control of me, I asked a local artist to teach me to draw. Drawing nature helped me focus on what was real. After introductions, she said, "Oh, it's such a beautiful day, let's sit under that cottonwood tree in front of your house." She retrieved two sketchpads and some pencils from a canvas bag, and said, "Now you sit down over there, and I'll find something for us to draw. She arranged a twig, ball, and mound of grass and said, "Imagine that this has a frame around it. Concentrate on these three figures."

I stared hard at the ball, grass, and twig while demons barraged me with obscene names. "Okay, she said," "look for areas of light and dark, and consider the relationship of the ball to the twig to the grass." We sat shoulder to shoulder and held a pencil to measure the objects. "See, the ball is twice as tall as the grass."

Demons flooded my body with terror, the kind one feels when a large man rushes toward you brandishing a machine gun. They taunted that unless I identified the correct height and width, they would severely punish me and make sure the artist never came back. Trembling, I steadied my gaze and willfully looked at the ball.

During the weekly lessons, we mostly talked about art, but she also shared stories of her family and friends at church. Under her gentle tutelage, I observed the forms, lights, and darks of nature, first in pencil sketches and then in pastel drawings. I leaned on the kindness of this Christian woman, whom God surely provided during this difficult season.

I carried my sketch pad everywhere, drawing mostly trees, flowers, and mountains. While standing in lines or watching my son at baseball, football, and judo, I sketched clocks, faces, and hands—anything that held my attention while the demons clamored at my insides. They made it impossible to relate to people in meaningful ways.

Some afternoons I rode my bike to the cemetery at the top of a hill where I could sketch the mountains. I put my pencil and pad in a backpack attached to my bike seat and pedaled on the paved paths winding through the rows of marble headstones. Freshly cut flowers adorned some of the manicured mounds. I stopped to read the names, dates, and messages engraved on the stones. LOVE IS ETERNAL, I read on one of them, and smiled wistfully wondering if love only existed in eternity.

One afternoon I stood next to a ten-foot marble column with a rectangular base about a foot in diameter and stared at the

Rocky Mountains. The mountains looked like a velvet blanket folding across the Front Range with green, brown, and black tones blending one to another. A brilliant blue background framed the massive mountains, which spread out as far as I could see to the right and left of me. Straight ahead I saw a thin, black horizontal line that I knew was the hogback, a jagged ridge traversing the base of the mountain. My eyes traveled up another thin vertical black line, which was a valley where streams filled riverbanks. My gaze rested on the whitened peaks ruling from behind. Here I paused, awestruck.

"Strong. Solid. So beautiful. You've endured for centuries," I said aloud. Saddened, I said, "I wish your strength could help me." Fearing that dwelling on such matters would plummet me to despair, I looked down, and my eyes fell on the message written at base of the obelisk. *Faith*. Instinctively, I moved on around the obelisk and read, *Faith, In God, In Yourself, In the Universe*. I went around a couple times, stopping to gaze at each word and repeating it aloud. I looked up at the mountains, down at the earth beneath my feet, and up at the sky. "There must be a spiritual source stronger than these spirits," I said aloud. "This evil cannot rule the world. How could beauty survive?" Sighing, I lifted my bike off the ground and nodded goodbye to my sanctuary. I felt most at home among the headstones and grassy mounds and returned often to read the words on the base of the obelisk.

### Summer 1986

The pitcher hurled the ball somewhere between the knees and chest of the ten-year-old batter who dug in at the plate. "Strr-ike!" the umpire bellowed, his hand jutting out sideways and his knee jerking waist-high. I sat behind the backstop with my pencil poised to record the stats on the Little League summer baseball team. Sometimes the ball pounded the fence about three feet from my face, and I always flinched when it did, but this time the catcher caught the ball, examined it to make sure it was suitable for play, and threw it back to the pitcher. Would he approach the pitcher for a conference? No, not this time.

The scorekeeper from the other side, sitting next to me, whispered, "Was that a strike?"

"Yes," I nodded, careful not to take my eyes off the game.

"What was the name of the batter?"

Suddenly my mind whirled and the spirits bombarded me with names, "Henry Larsen, John Holmes, Larry Wilson—what's the name, Sharon? Can't you remember? Are you so dumb that you can't keep track of something so simple as who's at bat?" Flooded with anxiety, I steadied myself and answered, "I can't remember. Let's see if we can catch his number."

"Can't remember the names of the guys on your own team?" She laughed and said, "Oh, he's number eleven. What's the name of number eleven?"

The spirits continued, "Can you at least remember her name, Sharon? It's Sally. No, is it Joan, Mary, Jean? Smile Sharon. Number eleven is Joe, John, Harry. Try to look normal."

"Guess you'll have to look it up; my mind's not working too well tonight," I smiled and continued to stare at the play.

"Strr-ike three!" The umpired yelled, "Batter up!"

I prepared to plot the play in the diamond-shaped box and thought, "Let's see . . . three called strikeouts get a circled backwards K."

"No, Sharon. It's a forward K," the spirits challenged as forward and backward Ks flipped through my mind. I pretended to look for someone in the bleachers until the confusion abated and then marked the play, a circled backward K.

The umpire cocked his thumb at the next batter, and my son, Michael, respectfully stepped aside. The ump then yanked a small whisk broom from his back pocket and bent to dust the bag, spreading his legs to allow room for his belly. Assured that both the runner on third and the pitcher had a clear view of home plate, he straightened up, shoved the broom into his back pocket, pulled at his pants, squared his mask, and shrieked, "Plaaay baaalll!"

Michael stepped to the plate. My heart sped up, and I hid my eyes. Whether my terror came from me or the spirits, I could not tell, but I did know that I wanted him to do well.

"Strr-ike!"

I checked the box. Crack! The ground ball spun between first and second, and Michael barreled toward first base. The second baseman scooped the ball and threw it to first as Michael arrived. "He's out!" the umpire yelled. My heart sank, but cheers erupted to my left, and I turned to catch the final plunge of the runner from third base. He crashed the catcher, who bravely blocked the bag and sent him head over heels into the dirt. The runner tripped over home plate and sprawled at the umpire's feet as the ball casually rolled to a stop between second base and the pitcher's mound.

Parents cheered and gave one another high-fives, and coaches and players pounded Michael's back in celebration of his run batted in. Michael beamed.

One parent, sitting in the bleachers to my right, yelled, "David, next time throw it home!" Then he smiled good-naturedly as a neighbor said, "He could have thrown it to third. That's what my son did last week."

Throughout the summer I saw a lot of these people at parent meetings, score-keeping clinics, and two or three games every week. Since spring 1982, when his father and I separated, Michael and I lived in the suburbs, and our home life revolved around getting to Scouts on time, attending ball games and practices, and participating in various school activities. I kept Michael active in sports and school, hoping people there could give him what I knew I could not.

I kept a close rein on the rage emanating from the spirits. Just expressing the slightest irritation while correcting Michael could suddenly plunge me into an enraged tirade, so I waited for the emotions to pass before saying anything to him. Consequently, I was more passive and less authoritative than was my nature, and I looked to other authority figures to fill in the gap until I could get my bearings again. Fortunately, Michael flourished under their tutelage.

Strange, I had spent the first twenty years of my adult life examining my inner life. Now I was using all my strength to deny it. The irony of my predicament never eluded me. Twenty years earlier I embarked on my journey of personal growth, never dreaming I would end up barely able to keep score at a Little League baseball game. Then I thought I molded my future, and I took my responsibility seriously.

Now that competent, confident person existed only as memory fragments and a vague sense of what was. I clung to her nonetheless to offset the lies that besieged me, "No, that's not me. No, that's not me," I asserted again and again each day. But no new thing grew within me.

The floodlights lit the emptied field as the boys gathered bats, balls, and bags. I tallied the score and snagged the coach to sign the sheet before walking up the hill to my car. Michael walked beside me and, with soft drink in hand, smiled a sheepish grin and said, "We won, Mom. Isn't that great!" I beamed back and wrapped my arm around his shoulders, "It sure is, honey. And to think you hit the winning run. I'm so happy for you." The floodlights shut off halfway up the hill, so we picked our way through the dark up to the church parking lot then headed home.

### December 1986

My friendship with Tad began in 1962 at the University of Iowa, where we both studied nursing. Her real name was Mary Claire, but her family nicknamed her Tad, a derivative of tadpole, and it stuck. Mainly we kept in touch through annual Christmas letters, but she did attend two training workshops I conducted in the mid-seventies and stayed at our mountain house during those times.

A psychotherapist like myself, Tad also abandoned her Christian roots, opting to become a Zen Buddhist instead. In a recent Christmas letter, she described a dramatic turn in her spiritual journey, but I could not remember how or where she ended up. December 1986, while attending a conference in Los Angeles, I called her at her home in Burbank.

"Hi, Tad. It's Sharon."

"Hi, yourself. It's good to hear from you. What are you doing in town?"

"Oh, I'm attending a conference."

"How are you doing, Sharon?"

"You really want to know?"

Tad paused and asked again, "Yes, Sharon, I really want to know. How are you?"

"Well, I'm not doing so well. You remember when I wrote about channeling spirits? Well, a couple years ago they turned on me, and I can't make them leave. I don't know what to do."

"What's it like?"

"It's bad, very bad, especially when I'm alone. They infuse thoughts and feelings into me and keep me awake at night. Sometimes my body is racked with pain, and yet I know nothing is wrong. The first year was the worst, but now they allow me to work. Otherwise, they interfere with my relationships, making it impossible to sustain a friendship. My life is not my own."

"Sharon, that's terrible. What are you doing about it?"

"I've tried many things. Spiritually, I simply try to meditate on truth and love, but mainly I stay busy. You know Michael's ten now. Well, he's in baseball, football, Scouts, and very active in school, and we live in a neighborhood full of good people. Then I have my practice." Embarrassed by the pathos of my situation, I laughed, "I trust your spiritual odyssey is going better than mine!"

"Yes, it is. I'm very happy." Then she added, "I know only one person who came up against what you are facing and came out okay. I'll send you his biography."

"Oh, that would be nice. I'd love to read it. Send me whatever you have. I don't know where to turn. I've learned to live as if it's not happening, mainly by remembering how I used to be. But it's like treading water. I can't go forward, nor do I want to give up. Surely the solution has to be spiritual. Don't you think?"

"I certainly do!"

"I knew you'd understand. Thanks, Tad. Look forward to hearing from you."

# CHAPTER 10

# Could Jesus Christ Free Me?

*Therefore God exalted him to the highest place and gave him the name that is above every name, that at the name of Jesus every knee should bow, in heaven and on earth and under the earth, and every tongue acknowledge that Jesus Christ is Lord, to the glory of God the Father. (Phil. 2:9–11)*

*God himself compelled me to seek Jesus. His Spirit was ushering me into his Kingdom. But how does one become a Christian?*

### January 1987

MY HEART SOFTENED IN A WISTFUL, almost melancholy way whenever I took my white Bible from the bookshelf and put it into a cardboard box to cart to my next residence, where I unpacked it and squeezed it back onto a shelf. I had acquired it at age fifteen after parroting back a mountain of verses from the Bible to our pastor. He presented it to me in front of the entire congregation, and after the service I opened the white box and lifted it from the white tissue.

No one could ever mistake the five-by-eight-inch book for anything other than the Holy Bible. Bound in white leather with a plain front and back, it had a tiny gold zipper that ran from top to bottom to protect the salmon-colored edges of the thin pages. Sometimes I fingered the gold of every letter etched on the side, H-O-L-Y B-I-B-L-E.

Five of the 981 pages contained colored pictures of prominent biblical figures of the Old and New Testaments. I smiled sympathetically at Joseph, who looked forlornly at his brothers as a caravan approached from behind. And at another, I warmed at the sight of Jesus holding a baby as older children surrounded him. And further on, Jesus sat under what looked to be an apple tree as he taught his disciples to pray. Someone had placed a card inside the front cover. It read, "The LORD bless thee and keep thee: The LORD make his face shine upon thee," which is exactly what our pastor said at the close of every Sunday service.

No pencil mark or careless creases marred the fragile pages—perhaps because I never read it. When ministers and some adults read from the Bible, the tone in their voice told me that only the knowledgeable or the highly religious could comprehend it. Certainly not me.

Nothing in my adult experience challenged my childlike perspective until Tad sent me the gray, hard-covered book. I read the title, Oxford NIV Scofield Study Bible, and my name engraved in silver at the bottom. I first thought, "Sure doesn't look like a Bible—more like a dictionary. But how sweet of her to think of me." Then I saw that Tad had tucked a note inside the front cover. It read:

*Dear Sharon,*

I've marked the section in the Bible that describes how my friend Jesus confronted an evil spirit. Also, I'm sending a book written by Johanna Michaelsen, who battled evil spirits. Give me a call after you've read them, and we'll talk more.

Love,
*Tad*


"Tad's a Christian? Amazing! Well, I'm glad she's found her niche."

I opened to the page Tad had marked with the yellow stick-on note and followed the arrow to a verse she obviously wanted me to read: "Jesus, full of the Holy Spirit, returned from the Jordan and was led by the Spirit into the wilderness, where for forty days he was tempted by the devil. He ate nothing during those days, and at the end of them he was hungry" (Luke 4:1–2).

"Well, I would think so," I thought. "The longest I've fasted is ten days, and I drank liquids. I can't imagine not eating or drinking for forty days."

I moved my finger down the page, "The devil said to him, 'If you are the Son of God, tell this stone to become bread'" (Luke 4:3).

Demons exploded anger within me. Who cares if he can turn a stone into bread—what does that prove? And I read on, "Jesus answered, 'It is written: Man does not live on bread alone.' The devil . . . " (Luke 4:4–5). A foreboding and loathing overcame me. I could read no further and closed the book. "Devil!" I thought. "Does anyone still believe in the devil?

And which Jesus are they writing about here anyway? The ascended master of the light, the one who channeled the Course in Miracles, the impostor who torments me, or is this the Jesus of the Mormon church, the one my mother tried to emulate?

"No. No," I said, stacking it with the other esoteric books beside my couch, "they're all masters of illusion!"

Then I picked up *The Beautiful Side of Evil* by Johanna Michaelsen. "Very apt title," I thought. Doesn't that say it all! Evil appearing beautiful. I carried it to my bedroom.

I sprawled crossways on the bed and opened the book. Sentences leaped from the page. I muttered aloud, "This woman understands. She knows."

I read, "I reached out my hand and with my fingertips lightly touched the image of the ancient Aztec warrior who was now Pachita's spirit guide . . . "[4] Yes, and that is how they hook us, I thought. I remembered how my spirit guides gained my trust. During a meditation class at the spiritualist church, the figure of an Indian had appeared in my mind's eye and identified himself as White Cloud, a Paiute chief. He offered to bring healing and wisdom through me to others. Shortly after, I saw a painting of an Indian in the window of a local art gallery. The full headdress of eagle feathers and weathered face replicated the man who appeared to me during my meditations. I asked to see the print and read on the back side that the figure in the painting was a Paiute Indian chief. Other spirits appeared to me over the years and pretended to be famous persons. After they introduced themselves to me and related information about their lives, verified their identity through recorded biographical data.

"And what actually did that prove? Mainly that they know information about famous people and ancient gods," I admitted dryly. "I bet they go from medium to medium with the same

---

4    Johanna Michaelson, *The Beautiful Side of Evil* (Eugene: Harvest House, 1982), 13.

stories, mesmerizing with facts and figures. And then once they have a person hooked, they dazzle with their magic tricks."

I read on, "who was now Pachita's spirit guide, the one by whom the miracles of which I had heard spoken were performed."[5] From the beginning, the spirit girl who conducted the development classes had instructed that supernatural powers never originated within me. Spirit created the images or visions, reflecting conditions in the past, present, or future as they tapped levels of consciousness unavailable to us because of our confinement in time and space. They said that during this incarnation, for reasons I never understood, I served as a conduit or medium for their expressions, just like Johanna and Pachita.

I read on. "Soft, low laughter began to echo in my head, a kind of laughter I had never heard before and which filled me with terror. . . . There are spirit beings all around us. I can see them, hear them. I feel when they are near calling to me, but sometimes I'm so afraid of them."[6]

"Yes, she understands." Her story unfolded to the climax when she asked Jesus Christ to be her Lord and Savior. Dumbfounded, I uttered, "What? She became a Christian? She actually takes the Bible seriously?" Although surprised, I believed her, but I just could not imagine myself doing that. "With so many powerful spiritual forces in the universe, how can I know which one is right for me?" As I attempted to read the last third of the book, which was loaded with Scripture, my heart raced in a mixture of fear and dread, and I could not finish it. I set the book on my nightstand and decided, "If the Christian Jesus turns out to be the way, then

---

5    Ibid., 13.

6    Ibid., 21, 52.

so be it, but I'm not going to rush into anything. I do know, though, that she got free, and so will I."

Quite miraculously the attacks lessened, that is, until April when the spirits again harassed me day and night. "It's getting worse," I muttered turning on my side to rest on my elbow. "This is terrible!" I mumbled and looked at the clock. "Three o'clock. Ten minutes of sleep each hour all night long. What are they doing? I won't be able to function tomorrow!" I rolled on my stomach, cupped my face in my hands, and massaged my temples. Then it happened. A wrath welled up and unleashed bullets of rage. Squaring off against the spirits, I yelled, "Enough! Enough!" Although stunned at my gall, I strengthened at each utterance, "Stop it! You're to leave me alone!" I felt no fear of them for the first time ever and suddenly, "Johanna. Remember Johanna. Become a Christian," cycled through my mind. Riding the crest of my newfound fortitude, I declared, "I'll become a Christian. I'll accept Jesus Christ."

I sobbed my relief and promised, "I will find a Christian. If Johanna can do it, then so can I." My course was set. I sighed and fell asleep.

The next day I called Tad. "Hi, Tad, it's Sharon."

"Hi. It's good to hear from you. Did you get the books I sent?"

"Yes, I did, and I appreciate your sending them to me. I've decided that I would like to become a Christian but wondered how you go about doing that."

"Oh, Sharon, I'm so glad. After we talked last December, I asked my pastor how I should advise you, and he said that you should walk into a church and tell them that you are demon-possessed and want to know Jesus Christ."

"Okay. You know, Tad, it just blows my mind that Christians believe in evil spirits, or demons, as you Christians refer to them. I had no idea. I thought Christians only focused on behavior."

"Oh, no. They very much believe in the supernatural. And really, don't be afraid to ask these kinds of questions. You'll be surprised at how the Bible answers them all." She paused and added, "I can't begin to tell you what a difference Jesus has made in my life."

"Well, I'm happy for you. I think it's right for me too. I'll look for a church. Thank you for your help, and I'll call if—no, when I get stuck," I laughed.

"Oh, please do. I'm here for you!"

"Thanks, Tad. Bye."

Within a week, I consulted a woman who specialized in releasing people from evil spirits. We met at an office in a community mental health center where she worked.

"First I need to know if you are a Christian," I said.

"Oh, yes, I'm a Christian," she said, her dark eyes smiling at me.

"Well, I'm demon-possessed, and I want to know Jesus Christ. Eleven years ago I became involved in the New Age and became a psychic medium, channeling five spirits. When I told them—the spirits I mean—that I no longer wanted to channel, they took possession of me and won't leave. Can you help me?"

"Yes, I think I can. My people refer to me as a *curandero*, and in our tradition, that is someone who communicates with spirits. I believe in Jesus Christ and attend church regularly and know I'm within the will of God. Otherwise, why would he give me this power?" She smiled and reassured me further. "I very much believe in spirits, and although I'm not possessed like you, they sometimes attack me. I'll tell you how to get rid of them."

"I would very much appreciate your help. I've had a hard time getting people to believe me. Most say that the voices originate in my mind, and others say that if I simply ignore them, they will go away. I had no idea Christians believed that spirits interfered in people's lives." Then I said, "I do need your help. Sometimes they make it difficult to complete even the simplest tasks."

"Yes, I know it gets real bad. Well, here's a ritual I want you to follow. First take three personal objects and place them in a triangle on your bed. These represent the Father, Son, and Holy Ghost. Then sit in the center and recite a Scripture. Do you know one?"

"Yes, I remember the Twenty-third Psalm. I can read it from the Bible my friend sent me."

"Yes, that would be fine. Soak a gold chain in oil in the afternoon sun and rub that chain on your third eye and stomach as you recite the verse. Then pray for the gentle spirits to come. Also purify your house by putting alcohol and salt in an aluminum pie tin, and light it with a match. If you do this, you needn't remove anything from your house associated with the occult." She confided that when attacked, she also tied a ribbon and repeated an affirmation as she fingered each knot. She said that if I did these things and continued to ignore the spirits, they would be gone within eighteen months.

As I turned my car into Denver rush-hour traffic, I recalled a vision I received while meditating several years ago. Three men, shrouded with long shawls, huddled around a glass beaker filled with a ball of bright light. Quite taken by the light, they raised their arms and, with robes flapping, clapped their hands and joyously encircled the beams emanating from the container. As the men danced round and round, the light lifted from the beaker and bounced around the small, bare room—off the ceiling, walls, floors, and, indeed, off the men themselves. But the men no longer gazed at the light and instead worshiped the beaker.

Immediately following the vision, the spirits then impressed upon me that the beaker in and of itself had no power and that it was fruitless to worship inanimate objects or engage in rituals if one lost sight of the essence of power. Power resided in spirit. Period. From this I deduced that rituals were useful in that they helped us focus our attention on a spiritual reality, but they were merely a vehicle for knowing that reality, and by themselves they were like empty vessels.

I thought of these things as I sat hemmed in on all sides by cars and pick-up trucks. There has to be an element of truth in what I've learned. Surely Jesus Christ can free me without necklaces, triangles, and burning salt. Seems strange that Christians rely on the same rituals as mediums and shamans. But if he releases his power through these practices, then who am I to question? I now moved at a snail's pace from one light to the next.

"Well, the bottom line is that Jesus Christ will free me," I said aloud. "I just have to find out how to get to him! I will find him. That I know. I will." I worked my way home.

I carried Tad's Bible to my bedroom and sat in the middle of the bed. I opened it to the Twenty-third Psalm and hesitated before reading it. "Should I form the triangle? It feels ridiculous." The demons held court in my mind, one side justifying why I should form the triangle and the other presenting their arguments against it. Helpless to decide, I lowered my head and prayed, "Oh God, please send your gentle spirits around me." Then I read, "The LORD is my shepherd, I lack nothing." Tears gently filled my eyes and spilled onto my cheeks. "He makes me lie down in green pastures, he leads me beside quiet waters." The page became a blur, and the depth of my ache frightened me, and I stopped reading, left the bedroom, and never completed the ritual.

Within a day a friend called at my office to tell me about an interview of the Rev. Erwin Prange, a Lutheran pastor, and Fr. Malachi Martin, a Catholic priest, on Oprah Winfrey's television show. The two specialized in exorcisms. "The priest said that time heals nothing and that you need to accept Jesus Christ as Lord and Savior and cleanse your house of everything related to the occult."

"Yes, but how do you do that? I mean, how do I become a Christian?"

"The Lutheran pastor said that you should go to the nearest church and tell them that you are demon-possessed and want to know Jesus Christ as Lord and Savior."

"That simple? Literally just walk into a church? You mean they don't have to have special skills in dealing with these things?"

"That's what they said. Go to the nearest church and walk in."

"Okay. That's what I'll do." So I did.

Within an hour, instead of eating lunch, I walked the block to a small, dark brick church. I walked up the ten steps, opened the tall door, and stepped into a semi-lit entrance area and stopped. As my eyes adjusted to the light, I noted a faint musty odor associated with old buildings and then saw off to my left and through double doors the backside of dark-brown pews. I wanted to peek in but hesitated. No, it feels like rummaging through someone's house uninvited. I turned from the sanctuary and noticed a door ajar down a hallway to my right. I gently knocked.

A pleasant-looking, thirtysomething man rose from behind a desk and approached with his hand extended. I shook it and introduced myself.

"Hello. I'm Sharon. Do you have a moment to talk with me?"

"Yes, of course. I'm the pastor of this church."

"Well, you're just the person I need to talk to. I'm demon-possessed, and I want to know Jesus Christ as Lord and Savior. Years ago, I became involved in the New Age and channeled five spirits. When I asked them to leave, they took possession of me, and they won't leave. So I want to know Jesus."

His gaze never wavered as he said, "Well, we have a very conservative congregation here, and I'm afraid you really would not fit in."

Incredulous, I asked, "Where should I go?"

"Well, I'm not sure, but I know that there are churches better suited for you than here. I'm just afraid you would feel out of place."

Instantly I knew that he was confused, either because I had not made myself clear or because the demons had scrambled his mind. I immediately stood, extended my hand, and said, "Well, thank you for your time. Good-bye."

Shaking my hand and smiling warmly, he said, "Best of luck to you."

As I exited the church, I spoke aloud to override the barrage of demonic hilarity: "No, the minister is wrong. He's wrong! Jesus Christ is the answer, and I will find someone who can help me learn how to be a Christian. I will find a church."

I ran the block to my office and left a message on Tad's answering machine: "Would you find out which churches in the Denver area believe in demons and who will help me become a Christian?"

That night she called me back. "Hi, Sharon. It's Tad."

"Hi, Tad. Well, I got stuck!" I laughed and related my afternoon adventure. "He was nice enough, but I don't think he understood what I was asking, and I didn't know how to make it clear. It just got very confusing, but these spirits do that all the time." Then I added, "I know Jesus is the answer."

"Yes, he is, and it's a shame that happened. I asked my pastor, and he gave me the name of a Presbyterian church in downtown Denver and also suggested calling the Episcopal bishop and the Vineyard Christian Fellowship. Make an appointment to meet with the pastors, and if you run into trouble, call me back."

"I'll call them first thing in the morning."

The next morning, I thumbed through the yellow pages for the Presbyterian Church and called. A lady answered the phone.

"Hello, Corona Presbyterian Church. May I help you."

"Yes, my name is Sharon, and I am demon-possessed and want to know Jesus Christ."

Without hesitating, she said, "Of course we'd be happy to help you. Let me see when our associate pastor can meet with you." She put me on hold for a couple minutes, and when she came back, she said warmly, "Yes, he can meet with you next Tuesday at three o'clock. So come to our church then." She finished our conversation by giving me directions to the church.

I then called the Episcopal bishop, and his secretary set an appointment for me to meet with him immediately following my time with the Presbyterian minister. "There, if these two don't work, then I'll call the third one," I thought as I hung up the phone. "But a week seems like a long time to wait to become a Christian. Maybe I should talk with the Lutheran pastor in St. Paul who was on the Oprah Winfrey show. He seems to know about these things." I paused and thought, "I really can't get on with my life until I become a Christian. Shouldn't that be the first priority in my life?"

Without hesitation, I answered, "Yes!" I called the secretary at the North Heights Lutheran church in St. Paul, made an appointment to see Pastor Prange on May 7, 1987, and secured a plane reservation.

# CHAPTER 11

# Jesus Christ Freed Me!

*"Everyone who calls on the name of the Lord will be saved"* (Rom. 10:13).

MY CONVERSION WAS MORE A PROCESS THAN EVENT. YET, THERE WAS A MOMENT WHEN I CONFIDENTLY DECLARED, "I'M A CHRISTIAN. I AM FREE!"

### May 1987

I LOOKED THROUGH THE RAIN-SPLATTERED taxi window at the blur of lights lining the freeway and recalled times when my family trekked the hundred miles to Minneapolis so that my father could "take care of some business." "How ironic that I should return here to become a Christian," I thought. An image of my childhood home popped into my mind—a white house perched on a hill encircled by apple trees—my insides warmed. "Maybe I could visit," I thought, and then I remembered that years ago a tornado had ravaged the area, seriously damaging our house. Some places are better left as memories, I conceded.

Cindy, the woman who had called to tell me about seeing Pastor Erwin Prange on Oprah Winfrey, traveled to St. Paul with me. She had participated in the classes at the spiritualist church and, as with me, her involvement there and in other occult practices had nearly destroyed her life. After hearing the show, she decided to consult the pastor.

We arrived late at night and were heading to a motel recommended by the church secretary. We were to meet with Pastor Prange at ten o'clock the following morning, which would allow us to catch a later afternoon flight home.

"In and out," I thought. "Well, at least I know the man understands and will help me become a Christian." I turned to Cindy and said, "What a clean, beautiful city this is."

"Yes, the mall was gorgeous."

"As a girl my family accompanied my father to Minneapolis on business trips, and I remember the cold. Their winters give new meaning to the phrase 'a conveniently covered mall.'"

"Do you know your way around?"

I laughed, "Heavens no. I have no idea where we are or will be. And tomorrow I won't know where we've been. Thank goodness the driver knows the motel."

"Well, I have my toothbrush, makeup kit, and nightgown tucked in my purse, so I'm good for one night," she joked. "The secretary said the church was close to the motel, but we must take a taxi there. She was so nice. They have been swamped with calls since the broadcast, but she said not to worry; the pastor will fit us in."

"Swamped! Doesn't surprise me, with so many people into this stuff. I'm even reading about it in the newspaper. Won't be long before consulting psychics and seeking altered states of consciousness will be as commonplace as having your teeth cleaned. Deadly," I said shaking my head, "absolutely deadly, and it wears so many disguises that people don't have a clue what they're dealing with." We stared silently into the black, wet night, careful to shield from the other the war that raged within.

Pastor Prange interviewed us for a half hour before ushering us into the church sanctuary, where he stood behind the railing in front of an altar and asked me to kneel on the red-cushioned step, "You become a Christian as you repent of your sins and ask Jesus Christ to be your Lord and Savior.

"Would you like to become a Christian?" he smilingly asked. I nodded, and he said, 'Then repeat after me: 'Holy Father, I confess that I have sinned against you, and I ask you to forgive me.'"

I repeated after him, "Holy Father, I confess that I have sinned against you, and I ask you to forgive me."

"I invite Jesus Christ to come into my heart to be my Lord and Savior."

And I repeated, "I invite Jesus Christ to come into my heart to be my Lord and Savior."

He placed his hands on my head and prayed for me, and my mind stilled. Then he counseled, "It is most important that you find a church in Denver, attend regularly, and learn about God as described in the Holy Bible." He raised the Bible to eye level, stared directly at me, and said, "This is the Word of God. Read it." He smiled kindly and further instructed, "When you get home, cleanse your house of all objects associated with your involvement in the occult these past years."

I nodded, thanked him, and asked, "Am I now a Christian?"

"Yes, you are now a Christian," he said. "God asks us to confess that we have sinned against him and to accept his provision, Jesus Christ. You now have a new landlord, and his name is Jesus. Yes, you are now a Christian."

I smiled and quietly walked out of the sanctuary into the midmorning sun. My friend had also asked Jesus Christ to be her Lord and Savior, and she joined me on the church steps. "Let's go home and find a church," I said. We called a cab and caught an early flight home.

Like a foot soldier mired in muck who hears the general's order, "Clean your foxhole!" and hollers back, "Yes, sir!" but has no notion as to the nature or purpose of the war he's engaged in, and further cannot even find his feet—so I stood in the center of my living room and uttered, "I'm a Christian."

I hauled the black, oversized leaf bag from room to room, dumping in the obvious occult books, an eagle feather, crystals, and art—anything that depicted God as nature. I dumped all written, channeled material, including what I had produced for my doctorate, into the bags and dragged it all to the living room.

The demons attacked with a vengeance: "Throw it all away, everything you own! Strip yourself bare! Maybe then we'll leave." I spied my couch, and they taunted, "Oh, remember when we bought that together? Get rid of it! Do it now or we won't leave!" My mind whirled, and I collapsed on a stuffed black bag, and as I held my head, they screamed, "We're your landlord!" I shook my head to counter their claims.

Determined to rid myself of all ties to the demons, I then inspected every room, searching for and seizing any artifact that might bind them to my house and me. But it was true that everything in my house had been bought under their influence, and to rid myself of it all would leave me bereft. "Does Jesus want me to do that? Does he?" I pleaded, "I'm willing, but what does he want of me? How will I know?"

I frantically began stuffing everything I owned in garbage bags: my salmon-colored comforter I had occasionally sat on while meditating, all jewelry bought since communicating with spirits, clothes I particularly associated with occult practices, computer disks, candles. Anything loose and not absolutely vital to my everyday functioning I piled in the middle of my living room, crying, "Jesus, Jesus, is this what you want? Which voice is yours? How can I be sure?"

The demons laughed hysterically. I retreated to my spiritual shelf and sensed a gentle, "Do nothing. Wait," counsel. Like the foot soldier mired in muck, I did not know my General—his character, purposes, or strategies. I sat on the bulging black bag and waited for Jesus to show me what to do.

Driving anywhere was a feat, but that was particularly true when making the appointment the following Tuesday with the Presbyterian pastor. Confusion reigned—wrong turns, missed streets, frantic stops. I trembled, and my heart raced as I swung my car into the church parking lot. I pushed the buzzer and, after the click, grabbed for the door too late. So I buzzed again, this time with my hand on the knob. It clicked, I grabbed, it opened, and I followed the ramp up to the church office, where a secretary greeted me. "You must be Sharon, yes? Sorry about that door and that it's necessary." I smiled as she continued, "Reverend Stark is expecting you. Want a cup of coffee? He'll be right with you."

"No, thank you, but perhaps some water?"

"Sure. Oh, here he is. David, this is Sharon."

A young, dark-haired man approached smiling and offering his hand. "Hello, I'm David Stark. Welcome. Come into my office. I've invited one of our prayer ministers to join us. I hope that's okay."

"Sure. I'm just glad to be here."

He motioned me toward three chairs tightly circled in front of a desk piled deep, and I sat down across from him and next to a woman with smiling dark eyes and short silver hair. He looked intently at my face and said, "Now, before we do anything else, we need to pray and ask our Father to guide and bless our time together."

They immediately lowered their heads and prayed, approaching God as if children talking to a loving Father.

Then with hearts wide open, they talked to him as if to a trusted friend and yet with a reverence reserved for the holy and sacred. I was awestruck, and their demeanor awakened a hunger within me, "Oh, to love like that!" I yearned, and tears promptly streamed down my face.

After they prayed, Reverend Stark took a tiny pamphlet from his shirt pocket and placed it on the Bible resting on his lap. Then he said, "Sharon, tell us what has brought you here and how we might help you."

"Years ago I became involved in the New Age and became a trance medium. When I decided to quit, the spirits would not leave, and I am now demon-possessed. I want to know Jesus Christ as Lord and Savior." They listened patiently for the next half hour as I further explained my situation. I concluded by saying, "So, I'd like to be free of this, and I believe Jesus can do it."

"Yes, Jesus Christ came to set us free. Would you like to know him?"

"Yes. I went to St. Paul a couple days ago and asked Jesus to be my Lord and Savior, but I don't really know what it means."

Reverend Stark picked up the tiny pamphlet entitled *Steps to Peace with God.* "Have you heard of Billy Graham?"

"Yes."

"This pamphlet comes from him, and you may take it with you when we're finished. It recounts what God did for us," he explained and opened the cover. "First, do you see this person standing alone? Now, as a therapist you know that many people in the world are lonely and scared; they want to feel peaceful but can't. Well, God knows this. In fact, he says in the Bible, 'I have come that they may have life, and have it to the full' (John 10:10b). You see, that is what God intended for us, but there is a huge problem."

He turned the page, and I saw a man standing on a cliff looking across a deep cavern at God. "God intended for us to know peace, but the Bible tells us . . . " Suddenly the demons unleashed their scorn of the Bible: "Naive, simple-minded, unthinking people read that book! The final word from God? What gives them the right to say?"

I strained to hear the pastor through their vulgar expletives and finally asked, "Would you repeat what you just said again, please?

"Yes, I'd be happy to. Are they bothering you?"

"Yes, but please go on."

"The Bible tells us that long ago human beings decided to separate from God, choosing to direct their lives without him, and when they did, they sinned against God, their Creator."

Through the barrage of voices, I heard Reverend Stark read, "For all have sinned and fall short of the glory of God" (Rom. 3:23). He further assured me, "So you see, we're all in the same condition—sinners in desperate need of a Savior. No one can do it alone. No one." I nodded. Though my mind remained captive, I detached from the turmoil, retreated to my spiritual shelf, and listened to Reverend Stark.

"But we try, don't we? The Bible says in Proverbs 14:12 that 'there is a way that appears to be right, but in the end it leads to death.' And I'm sure you're familiar with all the ways we try to make up for this separation from God. As you described, first you tried to fill the void through helping others, and then when that couldn't satisfy that deep hunger, you turned to philosophy and false religions."

I nodded, and he turned the page. I saw Jesus Christ stretched across the cavern, serving as a bridge between the man and God.

"Well, 1 Timothy 2:5 says, 'For there is one God and one mediator between God and mankind, the man Christ Jesus,' You see God knew that we were doomed without him, and he loved us so much that he sacrificed his Son on the cross."

Immediately the spirits bombarded me with images in my mind. I sickened at seeing a bloodied man hanging from a wooden cross, and my body revolted in deep loathing toward God for killing his Son. "They lie. They always lie," I thought, and yet I wondered why Jesus had to die in order for me to be set free. Immediately I sensed that in time I would understand.

Reverend Stark asked, "Are you okay?"

"Yes. It's just the spirits, but I know they lie. Please continue. I want to hear it all."

He smiled and said, "Sharon, God did this for you."

"I would never ask anyone to suffer and die on account of me."

"Oh, really none of us deserves it. It's because of his grace—unmerited favor—that we're saved from a life separated from God." Though clearly perplexed, I asked to hear more.

"Sharon, to be reconciled to our righteous God, we must accept his provision, Jesus Christ. The Bible says that 'If you declare with your mouth, "Jesus is Lord," and believe in your heart that God raised him from the dead, you will be saved' (Rom. 10:9). Jesus Christ saves us from much and we gain much! Look here," he said as he pointed to promises listed in the pamphlet, "peace, forgiveness, abundant life, and eternal life. That's a lot! Eh?" He smiled.

I smiled politely but privately dismissed the banquet of promises. I just want my mind back and the opportunity to run my life again. I asked, "What do I need to do?"

"You become a Christian when you confess your sins and ask Jesus Christ to be your Lord and Savior. Would you like to do that?"

Barely able to hear him for the turmoil in my mind, I nodded, "Yes. Do you want me to say the words again?"

"Yes, now that you understand a little better what God did for us, it would be good to say the words out loud."

I prayed, "Lord Jesus Christ, I confess that I have sinned against you. Please forgive me. I want you to be Lord and Savior of my life. Amen."

"Now let us pray together."

They bowed their heads, and so did I. The minister prayed aloud, followed by the woman who had prayed silently throughout our time together. It was then that Jesus Christ did what no other entity could do: He freed me. His Spirit filled the icy void at the center of me, liberating me from the demons' grip, and I leaped from my spiritual shelf rejoicing. Instantly I knew that I no longer struggled alone and that a spiritual force in the Person of Jesus Christ had saved me. It was finished.

Jesus Christ lived within, secured my soul, and promised to heal me from the inside out as I followed his lead. In that instant I also knew that the Bible was his voice and that I should give it authority over my desires, thoughts, feelings, and intuition all tangled in lies. I willingly agreed, for his was the only voice in me that made any sense.

I was free. Although the demons still had the ability to harass my mind and body, they no longer controlled me. The person of Jesus Christ lived within me and promised to protect and restore me. When or how he would do this no longer concerned me; I just knew he would as I followed him.

I cried hard. Holding my stomach with one arm and covering my face with my other hand, my ache erupted like a geyser. I sobbed my gratitude to Jesus. I cried for the devastation of my body and soul. I cried my relief—I had found the Savior of the world, Jesus Christ.

Reverend Stark continued to pray, and the prayer minister gently placed her hand on my shoulder, soothing me with promises of God's faithfulness to complete what he had begun in me. Quickly my grief turned to joy, and beaming through water-soaked eyes, I exclaimed, "I'm free! I'm free! Jesus freed me!"

The pastor's face brightened, and he spontaneously honored God, "Praise God! That's wonderful, Sharon. Praise God!"

"But do you think we could meet again? I have many questions. I've never read the Bible and don't know much about Christianity. And I don't know what to throw away and what to keep in my house. What do you suggest I do next?"

"I say slow down and savor what God has done," he laughed warmly, still celebrating the victory. "God says in his Word that angels rejoice when one sinner repents. The angels are rejoicing, Sharon, because you have found the way back to God!"

"That's nice," I said, relieved to learn that some angels actually served God, yet embarrassed that they would make a fuss over me.

"So, yes, let's talk about how to proceed. It would be good for us to meet every week. We will read the Bible together and share what it means to be a Christian. About cleansing your house, I would say get rid of those items you used in ceremonies or rituals, occult books, and anything that might tempt you to think in the old ways." He paused and added, "You know, this book, the Holy Bible, is our road map. It's the only one we need. We read it and listen to God, and then do what he says."

"Thank you. Thank you so much for your time. I can meet whenever you say. From here I go to the office of an Episcopal bishop who has also agreed to meet and pray with me. May I come to your church on Sundays, or should I go somewhere else?"

"Yes, join us on Sundays and wherever else the Lord leads you."

"Right now the silence in my mind is deafening!" I laughed. "Thank you again. I look forward to talking with you next week and seeing you Sunday."

I left the church smiling broadly, and in a stage whisper shouted to the world, "I'm a Christian! I'm a Christian!" My insides turned cartwheels as I drove to my meeting with the Episcopal bishop.

# CHAPTER 12

# Jesus Christ Guided Me

*Trust in the LORD with all your heart and lean not on your own understanding; in all your ways submit to him, and he will make your paths straight* (Prov. 3:5–6).

*God gave me exactly what I needed. I read the Bible, the Holy Spirit guided me, and what He said always agreed with Scripture. Jesus led me out of darkness—one step at a time. The body of Christ embraced me.*

### May 1987

THE SPIRIT OF GOD BURNED within me as I drove to my meeting with the Episcopal bishop. I had never talked with a priest, so my perception was secondhand—that is, I had heard about them through my childhood friend Dolores. I remembered that Dolores loved priests and that I loved whatever she loved. As a child I respected priests because they publicly declared their love of Jesus Christ by dressing in black and wearing a cross.

As I drove to my meeting with the bishop, I remembered sneaking into the Catholic church and being terrified a priest would catch me. I thought, "I wonder how much of what I believed as a child was true? What do Christians believe?" I knew now, firsthand, that Jesus Christ was the most superior presence in the universe, and even as I whispered, "Thank you, thank you," I was hungry to know more.

The Episcopal bishop sat behind a mammoth desk. He was attired in black with his white collar peeking through. His elbows rested comfortably on the arms of his leather chair, his fingers gently touching his chin. His dark eyes bored into me, causing sweat to trickle down my sides as I related my story. It did not take long for me to discover that he was a man of authority, and my request to see him was extraordinary—not part of his daily routine.

"How did you decide to call me?" he inquired.

"My friend in Burbank told me that you believed demons were real and that you would help me become a Christian, and so I called. Since then I have become a Christian, but I wondered if you could help me find a church where I would fit in. And would you counsel me on how to deal with my situation?"

He smiled graciously, "South Denver? I believe I know a church near your home where you would feel comfortable. But first, I've been curious as to why people seek help in the New Age. What draws them?"

His question surprised me, for I assumed he appreciated how difficult it was for ordinary people to be Christian— sacrificing themselves in the face of adversity and loving with no expectation of being loved. Why would a person choose it? But he asked sincerely, and I answered philosophically, "When people realize that their relationships and achievements can't satisfy the longings deep within, they seek help from the supernatural. New Age philosophy teaches that people can be all they were created to be and that a supernatural consciousness, which is a source of energy, wisdom, and guidance, is available to facilitate their spiritual journey."

"Interesting. And yet Christianity is the most supernatural of all the religions."

I simply stared at him. Again, how could he not know that being a Christian seemed more about rules and regulating behavior and conduct than supernatural phenomena? "Well, let's see what God wants to do here," he said, smiling warmly at me.

"I was wondering if you would counsel me on how to make these spirits go away. I understand I'm in for a real battle."

Then it was his turn to stare at me. Finally, he said, "Being a Christian is more about developing a relationship with God than making demons go away."

I stared back, camouflaging my desperation, and thought, "They have to leave. Except for this Presence within me, they dominate me. I can't develop a relationship with any one, let alone God."

He walked around his desk, searched, and then exclaimed, "Oh, yes, here it is!" and reached for a tiny silver cylinder. After unscrewing the lid, he dipped his fingers into the oil and made the sign of the cross on my forehead. As he prayed, the warm Presence inside me gently expanded. He stepped back and smiled broadly, "You're going to be just fine. Just fine. Now there's an Episcopal church near your home. Introduce yourself to the rector there, and tell him I sent you. Join a Bible study and attend the services. Yes, you're going to be just fine!"

I shook his hand, feeling a long way from "just fine" but knowing that my life had changed. Thank God.

I drove directly to the Episcopal church, walked into the office, inquired about their Sunday morning services, and introduced myself to the rector as he passed by, going from one meeting to another. Then I found the sanctuary.

My new home! I stopped midway down the center aisle to sit in the pew and gingerly lowered the kneeler in front of me. I knelt and prayed, "Oh, Father." Tears gathered in my eyes and flowed down my cheeks, "Oh, Father, I'm so very sorry. I didn't know . . . didn't know. Please forgive me. Please forgive me." And then I sobbed as I would Sunday after Sunday for the next few years. I cried with gratitude that he saved me from evil; I cried for the lost years; and most of all, I cried with regret for abandoning him as a teenager when I thought him not equal to the task of healing my broken heart. I cried because he loved me and was faithful not to let me go.

He heard me. I grew still in God's house, safe, out of harm's way, "Dear Jesus, please show me what you want from me. I'll do anything you say. Show me your way. I want to know you." His love warmed me.

I sat back in the pew and gazed at God's house. Sunlight shone through the stained-glass windows. It sparkled reds, blues, and yellows. A railing encircled the altar and podium, and a cross embroidered in gold on red velvet covered the altar where the Bible lay open. God's house was richly adorned. Here I felt safe. I hated to leave this sanctuary but knew I must.

The next Sunday, I stopped midway down the aisle of the sanctuary to again stare at the gold cross behind the altar. It stood on a small brown box resting on a shelf built into a red brick wall. White daisies mixed with feather ferns were beside it, and a glint of light shimmered off the gold. My heart quickened, and I mouthed, "Thank you, Jesus."

As my fingertips gently brushed the back of a dark wooden pew, my gaze fell on the large opened Bible held by a stand situated at the center of the altar. Two tall white candles flanked it and matched the marble altar with the letters IHS inscribed in gold on the front of it. My eyes danced from the cross to the Bible and my heart filled up. A polished light oak floor defined the area where the priest would stand, and the railing encircling it opened at the center. A dark blue pad covered a step beneath it.

I eased into the seat next to the aisle and looked at the wooden podium to the right of the altar. Two white oblong scarves draped down the front, and just above the fringe I saw more gold letters. The reddish-brown podium blended with the brick covering the walls behind and on both sides of the sanctuary, as well as the exterior of the Episcopal church. Dark wood beams crisscrossed overhead.

I sat still. I had arrived early and found two others praying in the sanctuary. Across the aisle and up two rows, a solitary figure rested her elbows on the pew in front of her and clasped her head in her hands. Her thin shoulders slumped forward, and her peppered gray hair covered the side of her face. Suddenly she pulled Kleenex from her pocket, wiped her cheeks, and resumed her prayers, "It's okay to cry here," I thought.

I watched the woman rise from the kneeler and slide back into the pew, "Thank you, Lord for bringing me here." Tears filled my eyes, and I pulled the kneeler down, slumped forward as she had done, and prayed.

"Lord, I'm so sorry." Tears flowed, "Lord, please forgive me." Shaken by the depth of my remorse, I opened my eyes, stared at the cross, and closed them again, "Oh Lord, I'm so glad to be here. I'm sorry." I approached him as my loving Lord, grateful he delivered me and grief stricken over my life.

A tap on my shoulder interrupted my prayer, and I looked into the pleasant face of a woman indicating she wanted to sit next to me in the pew. I raised the kneeler and let her by. The church was nearly full by now. A woman entered from a door behind the podium to light the candles by the Bible and the candelabra on either side of the stage. The understated beauty awed me, but more pronounced was the overwhelming presence of the Holy Spirit prompting me to honor Jesus Christ, my Savior and Lord.

Music blared from the organ behind me and people rose. I turned to face choir members dressed in blue robes with gray collars. The choir marched two by two down the aisle, singing "He is high and lifted up and his glory filled the temple." Trailing their processional were priests dressed in long white robes. One carried a large cross and another lifted the Bible overhead. I looked at the cross, the Bible, their joyful faces, and a fresh batch of tears tumbled down my cheeks.

"You freed me, Lord Jesus. Thank you for freeing me."

A priest opened with prayer. Then we sang and read from the Bible. Everyone knew what to do.

"I love this place."

Later in the service, the priest said, "Open to page 360 for the Confession of Sin." Then he knelt on the blue padded step and faced the altar. Bowing his head, he said aloud, "Most merciful God, we confess that we have sinned against you in thought, word, and deed, by what we have done, and by what we have left undone. We have not loved you with our whole heart . . ."

My heart ached. Though confident God had forgiven me, I said it again, "I sinned against you, Lord Jesus." Around the edges of my mind, demons continuously mocked my lament, but

I ignored them and cried to God. Someone more powerful now owned me, and, unbeknownst to me, was even then showing and empowering me to fight the spiritual battle.

"We are truly sorry and we humbly repent. For the sake of your Son Jesus Christ, have mercy on us and forgive us."

The words echoed in my mind: "Have mercy, dear Lord." Broken beyond what I could measure, the words in the *Book of Common Prayer* expressed what I could not.

"The peace of the Lord be always with you," the priest said, raising his arms skyward.

"And also with you," the congregation boldly responded and spontaneously embraced each other. The pleasant-faced woman gently squeezed my shoulders, "The peace of the Lord be with you." She smiled broadly as if welcoming me home, and I grinned like a school girl.

That night, I went to my bedroom with the intention of asking Jesus if using the *I Ching* offended him. The *I Ching*, or *Book of Changes*, was an ancient Chinese divination practice. I was introduced to it in 1984 by a Jose Arguelles, who supervised my doctoral studies. "It's more than an oracle," he said, "because it gives you information and personal guidance about spiritual energies affecting your life. Now let me show you how this works." He dug into his pockets and retrieved pennies, which he handed to me. "We throw pennies, observe how they fall, and consult the Book of Changes," he said. "Hold them, sit quietly, and ask yourself, 'What do I need to know?' Do not ask a yes or no question, but one that allows the *I Ching* to address the spiritual dynamics of your situation. After you decide, I'll show you how to proceed."

After a moment I asked, "How will my studies progress?"

"Good. Now throw the coins."

I did, and he drew lines on a piece of paper until six of them stacked up. Choosing his words carefully, he said, "The *I Ching* is telling you that some of your beliefs must be dismissed and you may feel turned upside down for a time. . . . Very unsettling times ahead. . . . But as you listen and are guided by divine wisdom and intelligence, good fortune and success will follow. You must go through this process to succeed." Staring intently at me, he said, "Get ready. It's going to be a spiritual roller coaster!"

The reading scared me, and a few months later, January 1985, the demons took control of my life. How throwing coins elicited such information bewildered me, but I knew that through the centuries people had tossed lots, coins, and yarrow sticks when making decisions. To me such foretelling substantiated that the spiritual realm contained seeds of our past, present, and future. I rationalized that such knowledge allowed me to better accomplish the purpose of my life.

What I did not know was that God hates all divination practices. "Anyone who does these things is detestable to the Lord" (Deut. 18:12). While yet ignorant of this, I decided to ask God whether this practice was acceptable to him.

Turning on the overhead light and the lamp next to my bed, I retrieved the *I Ching Workbook* and pennies from the bookshelf. I placed them in the center of the bed. Then I stood at the side of the bed with my hands at my sides, looking down at the book. Glancing upward, I asked aloud, "Does this offend you, Lord?"

Silence.

Intent on seeking his will and fully expecting him to answer me, I inched my way onto the bed and sat cross-legged in front of the book and opened it. I leafed through the pages, noting the Chinese letters at the top of each page and the headings

written in English for the sixty-four hexagrams. At the top
of the first two pages, I read The Creative and The Receptive,
which according to eastern religions were basic elements in the
primordial life force shaping the universe. Taking the book in
my hands, I again asked, "Does this offend you, God? If demons
aren't involved, is it permissible to seek your counsel in this
way?"

A fog of terror descended as a demon hissed, "You'll never
hear him . . . We control you."

Immediately I prayed aloud, "Lord Jesus, please tell me if this
offends you. Should I stop using it?"

The demons chattered, but I trusted that God would make
himself heard.

Pennies cupped in my palms, I opened my eyes and stared at
the book. Then I stilled.

The Holy Spirit simply said, "No." He gave no explanations,
and his voice was not audible, but I knew it nevertheless. I
was not to consult the *I Ching*. Immediately, I put the pennies
down and closed the book. Obeying him was more important
than understanding. In time I would know why he commanded
me so.

Dumping the book in a black garbage bag, I smiled as I tied
the top, "I heard you. You are my God!" Then phrases recited
by the congregation at the Episcopal church came to my mind:
"We believe." But I couldn't remember the rest. So I found the
*Book of Common Prayer*, which I had purchased that morning,
and thumbed through it until I saw the Nicene Creed. As I read,
certain phrases leapt off the page, "We believe in one God, the
Father, the Almighty, maker of heaven and earth, of all that is
seen and unseen."

"Yes, I believe in you, God. "

"We believe in one Lord, Jesus Christ . . . he ascended into heaven and is seated at the right hand of the Father."

I smiled. "Jesus reigns."

"We believe in the Holy Spirit, the Lord, the giver of life, . . ."

"The Holy Spirit lives in me. He'll lead me. I'm home."

I closed the prayer book and held it tight to me. Closing my eyes, I prayed, "You reign, Jesus. Thank God, you reign."

# CHAPTER 13

# God Equipped Me for Spiritual Battles

*Finally, be strong in the Lord and in his mighty power. Put on the full armor of God, so that you can take your stand against the devil's schemes* (Eph. 6:10–11).

*Demons continued their assault. Christ emboldened me with his Spirit, Scripture, and Christian witness of his victory over evil. Jesus taught me about himself while embattled.*

ONE SUNDAY, I DROVE TO the early service at the Presbyterian church and then immediately to the 10:30 a.m. service at the Episcopal Church, and home. I changed clothes, savoring the sweet taste of Eucharist wine lingering on my breath. "Oh, Jesus. Thank you, Jesus," I said, and then my head began to swim. The swirling gathered momentum until I was capsized in waves of nausea. I stumbled to the bathroom. My stomach expelled the cup of hot lemon water and whole wheat toast from breakfast and the wafer and sip of wine of the Eucharist. I heaved, holding my stomach during the violent retching.

The demons' cruelty always stunned me. "We'll bring you to your knees," they said, displaying their dominion over my mind and body. "We rule! We're king!" they screamed. They hammered to the brink, strong-arming me to acknowledge their presence. "See what we can do! You can't escape! We'll never leave. No one can make us—not even your Jesus." They muscled me, and I detached so as not to believe their lies, because I knew that the Holy Spirit, One greater than them, lived in me and in time this too would stop.

When Jesus became my Savior, the demons lost control, and we all knew it. Yes, they could attack my body, emotions, and mind, but I had been warned to expect this. The demons would have me believe that because they could hurt me, they still had dominion over me—that Jesus Christ was not who he said he was and that his Spirit did not live within me. But they lied. In fact, their ability to influence me had no bearing on my standing in the spiritual realm, and now I could fight back using the weaponry supplied by God: prayer and Scripture. I belonged to Jesus Christ now, and in time this harassment would cease. Christ had renewed my will and given me a relationship with God. Though they hammered me, I was in Christ.

"Call Carrie," I thought. She was the prayer minister at the Presbyterian Church who had offered to pray for me during times such as this, and I had put her number by my bedroom phone.

"Hello."

"Carrie, it's Sharon. They're attacking me now. Would you pray?"

"Yes, of course. What's going on?"

"I'm nauseated and throwing up."

"Is Michael with you?"

"No, he's at his dad's on Sundays. . . . They attack me like this when I'm alone and at night. . . . I usually handle these attacks myself. Talking about it seems to worsen my situation."

"Well, we know Someone who can take care of it. Let's pray."

She prayed as if bowing low before God, "Holy Father, we praise you. We worship you. We love you. You say in your Word that your enemies are a footstool under your feet, and we believe you. In the precious name of Jesus Christ and covered with his blood, we command these demons to loosen their control of Sharon's mind and stomach. Jesus Christ is her Lord.

"You say that when two or more of us pray in your name, we can be assured that you are present, and, Lord, we know you are here. By our will, we choose to obey you. We wish only to serve you. Teach us how to pray. Show us how we might please you."

As she continued praying, the demons released their hold, the nausea subsided, and I breathed deeply. I served a victorious Savior.

"Thank you, Carrie, I feel better."

"Oh, I'm glad. God is so faithful. I want to give you a Scripture to repeat out loud during attacks." She leafed through her Bible, then said, "Yes, this one would be good. Do you have your Bible?"

I reached for my gray Bible on the nightstand next to my bed, "Yes."

"Turn to Romans. It's in the New Testament. First we have the four gospels—Matthew, Mark, Luke, and John—then Acts, then Romans. Find it?"

"Yes. Got it."

"Good. Now turn to Romans 8:1 and read it to me."

"Okay. Therefore, there is now no condemnation for those who are in Christ Jesus, because through Christ Jesus the law of the Spirit who gives life has set you'" (Rom. 1:1–2).

"Sharon, God loved us so much that he sent his Son to die on the cross, rise from the dead, and sit at his right hand. He gave us his Holy Spirit to reside within us. What a gift! He knew that we could never please him by relying on our natural talents and inclinations." She paused, turned pages, and continued.

"In another verse he reminds us, 'For it is by grace you have been saved, through faith—and this is not from yourselves, it is the gift of God— not by works, so that no one can boast.' You can find that verse in Ephesians 2:8–9. Essentially that means that nothing we do makes God love us any more or less. All he asks is that we accept his gift, Jesus Christ, and then love and obey him. He does the rest." Her voice full of conviction, she said, "Jesus Christ is a victorious King!"

Carrie's undaunted faith in the victory of Jesus buoyed me, "You know, in my spirit I know that to be true, and I've learned not to believe the confusion in my mind."

"I know. Satan hates to lose and will battle for your mind. His goal is to destroy your faith in God. But he is a defeated foe. God commands us to walk by faith—faith in Jesus Christ and his victory over darkness. He will lead you out of this as he does us all."

"I believe it, and I'll read Romans 8:1 today. Any others?"

"Yes, read Ephesians 6:10 to the end of the chapter. I'll find some prayers for you to read when alone and give them to you Tuesday when we meet. Please call when the seas get rough!" she laughed warmly.

"Thank you, Carrie. See you Tuesday."

I sat on the floor resting my head against the comforter and clutching the opened Bible in my lap. I prayed, "Thank you, Jesus, thank you."

The hours, days, months, and years spent staring at dramas from my spiritual shelf had trained me well for the warfare I now engaged. I knew how to detach when in the throes of confusion and torment, and I now had Jesus, trustworthy and true, to whom I could turn. No matter that Scripture sometimes baffled me and contradicted most of what I had based my life on. I knew in my spirit that God's words had more validity than anything that transpired within me. I pledged to abdicate my thoughts and emotions to him, giving Scripture authority over what occurred within me. If my thought life and emotions refuted the Bible, then I assumed I erred, and I would search God's Word for what was true and supplant it in my mind.

"I need a crash course in Christianity," I said aloud to myself. I opened my Bible to Ephesians 6:10 and read aloud: "'Finally, be strong in the Lord and in his mighty power. Put on the full armor of God so that you can take your stand against the devil's schemes. For our struggle is not against flesh and blood, but against the rulers, against the authorities, against the powers of this dark world and against the spiritual forces of evil in the heavenly realms. Therefore put on the full armor of God, so that when the day of evil comes, you may be able to stand your ground, and after you have done everything, to stand'" (vv. 10–13).

I paused, "How well I know. Nothing I've ever read so aptly describes my situation. I'm completely dependent upon Jesus Christ to free and protect me from these powers. He tells me when I'm under siege to put on his armor and stand—simply stand—and he will do the rest. I can do that." I read on: "'Stand firm then, with the belt of truth buckled around your waist, with the breastplate of righteousness in place, and with your feet fitted with the readiness that comes from the gospel of peace. In addition to all this, take up the shield of faith, with which you can extinguish all the flaming arrows of the evil one. Take the helmet of salvation and the sword of the Spirit, which is the word of God'" (vv. 14–17).

I restated aloud what I had read: "The Word of God is my defense, my sword. I align my mind with Scripture, God's truth, and then I'm in step with Jesus Christ, like a soldier in his army. Simple enough," I said to reassure myself, knowing full well that it was much simpler said than done. "And my faith in Jesus Christ shields me from the Enemy's arrows. Demons fashion the truth to serve their purposes, and my mind right now is useless when it comes to discerning spiritual truths, so I put my faith in Jesus Christ and the authority of the Holy Bible. Period!"

I read on: '"And pray in the Spirit on all occasions with all kinds of prayers and requests. With this in mind, be alert and always keep on praying for all the saints" (v. 18).

I smiled and closed the book. "Yes, prayer is key. Soldiers of Jesus Christ pray for one another. Okay. I'll pray, immerse my mind in Scripture, and put my faith in Jesus." I promptly typed the verses from Ephesians and made copies, attaching them to the mirror, nightstand, and kitchen counter.

The Tuesday after my Sunday call to Carrie, I met with her and Reverend Stark for instruction and prayer in a conference room at the Presbyterian Church. After prayer and discussion, David gently said, "You disobeyed God when you served as a channel and practiced other forms of divination or fortune-telling. In Deuteronomy 18:10–13, the Lord says, 'Let no one be found among you who sacrifices their son or daughter in the fire, who practices divination or sorcery, interprets omens, engages in witchcraft, or casts spells, or who is a medium or spiritist or who consults the dead. Anyone who does these things is detestable to the LORD; because of these same detestable practices the LORD your God will drive out those nations before you. You must be blameless before the LORD your God. ' You see, he really hates these practices."

"Detestable. He hates them!" My eyes widened, and I shuddered as the word *detestable* stung me. Suddenly I comprehended how severely I had set myself against God and thought, "Surely being a medium is the ultimate affront to God!"

David continued, "God hates all forms of divination, and as you know, it's nothing to fool around with. But God is gracious. When we confess our sins, he forgives us because of Jesus," and he said it again: "because of Jesus and what he did for us on the cross. Do you understand?"

"Yes, mostly. I think so. I understand that I'm in Christ, and that he alone saves me, not only from Satan, but from myself as well. I must confess my sins in order to be in close relationship with God."

"Yes, and what is true for you is true for all of us." David stopped and pulled a paper from his Bible. "Now, on this sheet you see a list of occult involvements. Mark the ones you participated in, and after you do, we'll pray."

I read them all, checked three-quarters of the list, and said, "But there are some not listed here. Should I add them?"

David laughed and said, "Yes, let's get them all taken care of!"

"Okay. I'm ready."

"Now move down the list and pray aloud, 'Lord, I sinned against you when I and then fill in the blank. 'I confess this as sin and renounce it. I ask that you forgive me.' If you have any other associations as we pray, that is, if the Lord brings other activities or people to mind, then confess and renounce them as you feel led. Carrie and I will pray with you."

I closed my eyes, lowered my head, and prayed, "Lord, I sinned against you when I channeled spirits. I confess this as sin and renounce it. I ask that you forgive me." Egglog's face flashed in my mind's eye; then Seth's, Starlight's, and others with whom I had talked paraded through my mind. As I saw them I spoke their names out loud and asked God to forgive my involvement with them. Next the face of Donna appeared, the medium who conducted the classes, and I prayed, "I confess that I listened to Donna. I renounce everything I learned from her and the spiritualist church. I confess that I attended various seminars and workshops pertaining to the occult and counterfeit spirituality and that I consulted mediums and healers. Please forgive me." I rummaged through the past eleven years of my life asking forgiveness for my involvement with various people, activities, and divination practices, including the Ouija board. When finished with the list, I looked at David, who encouraged me saying, "Good! You're forgiven! Any more?" I quieted my mind and silently asked God what else he would have me confess, and my childhood spirit friends came to my mind. I said to David, "I want to confess my conversations and reliance on the spirits I saw as a child."

"Go ahead."

"Lord, I want only to hear your voice, and I confess that I have talked with spirits that are not of your kingdom. I did this as a child and as an adult, and I ask you to forgive me. I renounce everything I learned from them and ask that you fill my mind with your truth."

David continued praying, "Lord, we ask that you release Sharon from all evil spirits associated with her family, specifically her mother. Please send them away, Lord. Free her."

My mind cleared, and I breathed a deep sigh, "I feel as if a great burden has been lifted from me. Long list, huh? You know, I had no idea these involvements were sinful. No idea."

"Oh, I believe you! And you are no worse a sinner than I am. We all need a Savior; none of us pleases God on our own. And don't think you have to confess everything you've done wrong in your entire life, just those offenses God brings to mind while in prayer. You'll learn to hear his voice."

"When I'm quiet I can tell the difference between God's voice and that of Satan. God's direction is gentle and firm and resonates with the Spirit within me. I feel safe and peaceful as I obey. But Satan's voice is urgent, accusatory, and domineering, like if I don't obey, I deserve punishment. With Satan I get the feeling that what I do and who I am is never good enough and what he wants most is for me to not exist." I paused. "I can't begin to tell you the difference between the two kingdoms. God's love for me feels endless; he wants me whole, healed, fully the person he created. The Holy Spirit is indeed the most marvelous gift I've ever known."

David's eyes grew misty, we prayed, and he closed our meeting. "Next time we'll talk more about forgiveness, that is, the people you need to forgive. I think we've done enough for today."

Before I became a Christian, I thought forgiveness meant learning to "walk in other people's shoes" so as to better understand them. Then I would say to myself, "Given the circumstance and who they were at the time, I can understand why they resorted to that. I mustn't pass judgment on them." But since receiving God's unmerited favor, I sensed that what God had in mind encompassed much more. Usually it was he who prompted me to forgive someone, and when I did, his sweet Spirit moved me to tears and I felt lighter. The more I forgave people, the less the demons harassed me and the closer I felt to God.

I began to see that forgiveness—God's for me, and mine for others—was the heart of the gospel and the key to getting free, so during my morning prayer times I regularly asked, Is there someone I need to forgive, Lord?

One morning as I prayed, I remembered my mother as she appeared the last time I saw her, Thanksgiving 1984. Mother stood in front of the steps of her yellow wood-frame house on a sidewalk bordered with brown grass that spread through cracks beneath her feet. A gray sky threatened snow. Her unbuttoned beige wool coat and cotton dress hung down her ninety pounds to mid-calf. A solitary figure, she braced her arms against her sides and clasped her hands in front, and with white hair framing her angular face, head cocked, and smiling, she struck a suppliant pose as if awaiting inspiration, so she would know what to do next.

I cupped my forehead with my hand and whispered, "Mother, you tortured soul. You turned to a false prophet and lost yourself." Tears flowed unchecked down my cheeks, and I sighed, "Oh, Mother, I forgive you." When I said it, my heart opened, and in that moment my estrangement from her vanished. I could imagine sitting next to her, taking her in my arms, and embracing her with the love of Christ.

At the suggestion of the rector at the Episcopal church, I attended a weekend renewal conference for the diocese in the Colorado mountains. After depositing my belongings in a dormitory-style room, I ventured into the dining hall, where a couple hundred people hugged, shook hands, prayed over food, ate, and listened intently to others.

Pushing my tray past the spread of glazed rolls, Jell-O, white bread, bologna, coffee, and red meats, I forked a slice of white cheese and scooped the tossed salad onto my plate, "What am I going to eat this weekend? I should have brought food," I said to myself, sprinkling lemon juice on my salad.

"Do you have any whole-wheat bread?" I asked the woman behind the table.

"No, sorry, nothing that healthy," she laughed. I smiled and moved on down the line.

"Do you have some hot water for my lemon juice?"

"No, just coffee and Kool-Aid tonight," the man behind the table answered and smiled. The demons laughed uproariously.

Shaken, I sat at an unoccupied table and prayed, "Jesus, I can't do this. Help me. Help me, please. It's too hard to be alone in this crowd. Let me go home. I'm too different. Help me, please." Tears threatened to embarrass me, and I gazed intently at my food.

"May we join you?"

Four women close to my age smiled brightly at me, and I said, "Sure."

Two sat next to me and two across. "We come from Durango, Colorado, and we're daughters of the King," one said and giggled.

"Cheryl, come on. She'll think we're nuts!"

"Okay. I'll be good. We've been marveling at how wonderful it is to be a daughter of King Jesus." She smiled and then asked, "We come to this conference every year. How about you? Where do you come from?"

"I'm from Denver."

"Which church do you attend?"

"Christ Episcopal, but I'm a new Christian."

They lit up. "Really! Cause for celebration! Welcome to the kingdom! How wonderful."

"Yes, I'm thrilled. But I don't know anyone here."

"Oh, you will. Please, would you sit with us during the conference?"

"That would be nice," I said, grateful beyond words.

"The first meeting is in the large hall after dinner. Hundreds attend, you know! It's going to be wonderful! See you there."

The hall teemed with laughter, music, and "Hi, so glad you're here! How nice to see you!" I scanned the crowd for my friends, and in spite of the din and commotion, spotted them smiling, waving, gesturing toward the seat saved in the middle of their row. Squirming past their raised arms and sweet songs, I stood alongside and joined the chorus of hundreds singing their praises to Jesus Christ. We followed the lead of a handful of men and women on stage playing guitars and singing their adoration.

"God inhabits the praises of his people. Let us lift our voices to him, inviting his presence to be among us. Let us worship our Lord!" the leader shouted.

Through tears of joy, I abandoned my reserve and sang love songs to Jesus, sandwiched by people who loved him as I did. I opened my mouth and heart, thanking God for bringing me to such a wonderful place.

The bishop, the one who had dipped his fingers in oil and painted the sign of the cross on my forehead, stood on the platform, raised his arms, and reverently prayed, "We love you Jesus. We praise you Jesus." Yes, he loved him too. These passionate eruptions within me were good, not to be squelched. It's the way Jesus wanted me to be—to love him with my whole heart. My shameless display of adoration pleased him. In fact, he wanted more.

The next morning as I listened to the speaker talk about our need for God, tears welled up in me, "Yes, Lord, without you I am nothing. My only hope resides in you." I looked at the sea of scrubbed-clean faces around me and added, "But Lord, though I confessed my sins with David and Carrie and you say I'm forgiven, I still feel like the worst sinner in the room! No one here has offended you as badly as I have."

Sunday morning at the closing ceremonies of the renewal conference, we celebrated by taking Communion, singing praises, and reading Scripture. The sweet taste of the Eucharist wine still filled my mouth as I sang, "Jesus, O Jesus, come and fill your lambs. Jesus, Jesus, come and fill your lambs." As I whispered his name, suddenly his presence bubbled up like a fountain within me, and buoyed by the power of his Spirit, I spontaneously said his name, "Jesus, Jesus, Jesus."

I fell to my knees sobbing, "It's you. Jesus. You pushed them aside. I can know you. Thank you. You are stronger!" I cried. "You'll set me free—completely free—and I now know how. By your Spirit! You are indeed more powerful than any demon. By your Spirit, you'll set me free. Thank you, Lord. Thank you, Jesus."

The woman next to me gently put her hand on my back as I cried my gratitude to Jesus. He had addressed my deepest concern: Would I be able to hear his voice even when not quiet and in prayer? Would I be able to discern his Spirit from the competing ones as I lived my life? His answer? Yes. Yes, the God of all creation, more powerful than anything in heaven or on earth, had made himself known to me.

I knelt, fully present, filled with his Holy Spirit. This was so different from channeling demon spirits who superimposed themselves over me. With them I vacated myself, detached as in a trance, so that they could use my mouth and mind as instruments for their communication. When the Holy Spirit filled me, I remained fully myself, alert, in control, yet willingly yielded to the power of his Spirit. Nothing that occurred violated my will or what I desired to do. By the power of his Spirit, I praised Jesus and prayed, "Lord, I will follow the lead of your Holy Spirit. Thank you for making yourself known to me. You are my God. My God!"

My friend Tad had sent three cassette tapes, which she labeled "Combat Praise." On them she had recorded various Christian groups, and their praises accompanied me all the way home from the conference. The demons mocked, screamed, taunted around me, but Someone lived within me, greater and more powerful than them, and I knew it. The Holy Spirit filled me, and I rejoiced!

# CHAPTER 14

# Why Did Demons Harass Me?

*No, in all these things we are more than conquerors through him who loved us. For I am convinced that neither death nor life, neither angels nor demons, neither the present nor the future, nor any powers, neither height nor depth, nor anything else in all creation, will be able to separate us from the love of God that is in Christ Jesus our Lord* (Rom. 8:37–39).

*Demonic harassment did not diminish my confidence that Jesus Christ would complete what he had begun in me. One day my mind would be quiet! But what part did I play in my deliverance?*

### August 1987

WHEN YOU'RE SLIPPING OFF A cliff, your wits a proven failure, and God holds you steady with his hand, everything you have seen, read, or believed about how life works suddenly turns upside down. Thus disposed, I dangled from his hand, confident that nothing could hold me except him. It was mine to cling, his to sustain, and the longer I clung, the more I learned about him. "Now faith is confidence in what we hope for and assurance about what we do not see" (Heb. 11:1).

Mornings, I sat on the beige couch in front of the tall windows with their mounds of evergreen shrubs, wrote in my journal, read the Bible, and prayed. During these times, Jesus was as real to me as if standing before me smiling, holding out his hand, and saying, "Follow me and don't be concerned when your mind betrays you and your body registers feelings contrary to who you remember yourself to be. I am the Truth, and you can trust me to lead you out of this." During these morning meditations, I could not hear, touch, see, smell, or taste him, but I knew his presence and what he wanted of me. I listened and obeyed, and as I did, God dipped his finger in balm and began to heal my body and soul.

Suspended and dangling, I waited for God to remove the demons completely and return me to firm ground so that I could function as the human being I had known before taking the dreadful detour. I fashioned her to be a good person, and I liked her. For when assembled, she was self-reliant, resourceful, steadfast, and responsive to the needs and feelings of others—traits I valued. But she lay splattered, strewn about like debris in a landfill. I wanted her back again. I did not know that God never intended to restore me, but rather desired to change me into someone who could reflect his nature.

When I was a child, my father had given my brothers and me a penny a day for each year we were old, a formula he borrowed from President Truman, who, Father said, used the method to calculate his daughter's allowance, "Just proves that God gave everyone some sense," he teased, implying that it was probably the only good idea that Truman ever had.

Though I received a week's allowance at a time, I allocated eleven cents a day to spend five for an ice cream bar and six for chewing gum or hard candy. Monday mornings I followed my brothers across the street to the grocery store, fingering and jingling my money in the pocket of my shorts. My brothers spent all they had within the first few days. Six-year-old Greg spent his forty-two cents on bubble gum and hard candy, and nine-year-old Tom splurged his sixty-three cents on Popsicles and gum. Toward the end of the week, overtaken by pity and guilt, I shared the least favorite of my stash with them, but never my ice cream bar.

One August afternoon, when the Nebraska humidity wilted us all, my father and brothers lounged on a couch in front of the air conditioner, and I collapsed across from them. I ran my tongue from one end of a vanilla bar to the other and back down again, slurping every drop that threatened to drip to the maroon chair. Greg sat forward and followed every lick with wanting eyes.

"It's not nice to eat in front of your brothers. You should share," my father scolded.

Stunned, as if he had slapped me, I thought, Surely he doesn't expect me to share my ice cream bar! Not this! "But they never have money, Dad," I whined. "I saved for this."

"Then you could buy them one. You should share."

"But I'd have nothing left for myself."

Frustrated, he said, "Sharon, eat it outside."

I sat on the back porch steps, licking and wondering how good people ever got anything for themselves and concluded that they must do it in secret so as to not make others feel bad.

When I was a child, I reasoned that I became a good person by giving to others, treating them kindly, and being fair in my transactions. I also believed that if I was kind, then I had every right to expect kindness in return. If I did no harm, then no harm should befall me. And if I found pleasure and hurt no one in the process, it was my right, my due, just and fair. Later, as an adult, I further reasoned that the sincerity with which I pursued goodness and truth should somehow protect me from harm. My efforts should be rewarded, if not by God, then certainly by others.

But even while so managing myself, asserting this modicum of control, I never truly addressed the fact that the way I envisioned the world had nothing to do with how it really operated. And now my abject reliance on God for any good thing confirmed these suspicions and debunked everything I had based my life on, exposing my suppositions as myths, vain imaginations. "All of us have become like one who is unclean, and all our righteous acts are like filthy rags," I read in Isaiah 64:6. Humbled, it dawned on me that pleasing God was what mattered, and my good deeds were to him like filthy rags when not in accord with what he wanted. God wanted me close, worshiping and honoring him, and when I was there, he transformed me into his goodness—something I could never do on my own. But I must do so willingly and seek him with my whole heart.

Mornings, I sat like a child at the feet of the personification of all holiness, righteousness, justice, and power—more than my finite mind could fathom. How ironic that at forty-five years of age I should be clinging to my heavenly Father's hand, more a child than when I was one, totally incapable of doing anything noteworthy, good, or deserving of reward. "I think he wanted me here all along," I said and read from Proverbs 3:5–6, "Trust in the LORD with all your heart and lean not on your own understanding; in all your ways acknowledge him, and he will make your paths straight."

With his ember burning inside me and fully confident that he would direct and sustain me, I decided to learn as much as I could about God, both from his Word and from the churches in the Denver community.

With two friends, I visited one church that held services in a renovated warehouse where five hundred folding chairs had been set in rows around a platform. The platform held two electric guitars, a drum set, a keyboard and stool, and a podium. A mammoth green tree stood next to a banner that proclaimed, "Jesus lives!" draped across the back wall. Two hundred or so singles, marrieds, and groups of young and old began arriving at about 6:45 p.m. for the 7:00 p.m. service, which was scheduled to end at 9:00 p.m. but lasted as late as 10:00 p.m.

The praise singers mingled up front, conversing in low tones and fidgeting with the microphones. "They'll sing the first hour," my friend said, "and then the pastor will deliver his message. Following his sermon, the prayer ministers pray for people in the congregation. They have trained counselors here. Since my weekend renewal, I felt best when praising God and praying to him. I came because I had been told that people here loved to worship God and specialized in a deliverance ministry, that is, praying in such a way that people were released from the attacks of Satan.

I loved to worship! Again, the tears flowed, my heart burst with joy, and I raised my arms and shamelessly sang of my love for Jesus. I felt safe, protected as I praised him. Fears vanished, voices ceased, and my heart filled with love. We sang for an hour before the preacher delivered his message. He held the Bible over his head and said, "This is our authority," and spoke about how God transforms lives. When finished, he said, "It is now time for us to pray for one another, but before we do, I sense that Jesus wants to talk with us tonight. Let's all stand and close our eyes. Jesus is going to communicate with you tonight. He'll appear in your mind and talk to you. Open your hearts and minds, and allow him to come close to you."

Then he prayed, "Father God, you say we are in Christ and have authority over the Evil One, and so now we take that authority, and in the name of Jesus Christ and by the power of his Holy Spirit, I command Satan to leave these people alone. The blood of the Lamb be over their minds. Amen.

"Now release your minds to Jesus. Let him come to you." I panicked at the prospect of giving any credence to visions and thought, "Why encourage anyone to talk with God in this way?"

"I can't do this, Lord," I prayed.

The pastor continued, "Step out in faith and allow the Lord of the universe to show you how much he loves you and wants to protect and guide you. The blood of Jesus be over your mind."

I wrestled, "Oh God, do you want to show me that you have dominion here too? That you speak to me through visions too? Is this what you want me to learn now? Even as I hesitate, do I disobey you? I'll do whatever you say."

"Now raise your hands if you see the Lord," he said, and hands shot up all over the room.

I closed my eyes and prayed, "All right, Jesus, I give my mind to you. Reveal yourself to me. Show me your way." Instantly a beautiful angel appeared in the place in my mind where I had seen so many visions through the years, and he spoke to me telepathically, "Jesus sent me to give you this message. 'Your time of torment is over. The spirits now must leave, and you will know the peace that comes from Jesus.'" I heard the pastor say, "Good, more of you are seeing Jesus. Trust it. Embrace what he says. Don't back away. Thank him. Praise him."

The angel silently stood in front of me, bathing me in love and what felt like healing energy, and I cried my gratitude, "Thank you, Jesus! Thank you." Turning to my friends, I said, "They say it's over. Over! My mind is clear! My mind is quiet!"

"That's wonderful, Sharon."

The praise team led us in our closing songs, and we went our separate ways. "I'm free. He promised he would free me, and I'm free!" I cried and sang all the way home.

I slept like a newborn until 2:00 a.m. I awoke, and the beautiful angel appeared in my mind's eye, loving and reassuring me that the time of torment was over. Suddenly my body stiffened in fear, the angel vanished, and I heard, "Sorry we had to fool you, but you see, we are never leaving. You will always be ours. Did you really think we'd go away? Not even your Jesus can make us leave. Want some visions, Sharon?" they mocked. Numbed and dazed, I stared at the tree limbs swaying in the moonlit night as they ranted, "Don't think you're safe because you say your special words. No sleep tonight, Sharon. Stupid Sharon. So sorry we have to hurt you, but you should have known better, and now we have to punish you."

Shaking my head at their lies, I realized that the angel had come from Satan, not Jesus. I leaned on my elbow and pulled myself upright on the bed. I turned on the light and a Christian radio station and draped the comforter around me as I slipped from the bed and huddled on the floor beside it. I took the Bible from the bedside table and opened it to Romans 8:1 and read aloud, "'Therefore, there is now no condemnation for those who are in Christ Jesus.' Yes," I said, "God loves me. God loves me. He would not punish me like this for mistaking one of Satan's angels for his. 'Through Christ Jesus the law of the Spirit of life set me free from the law of sin and death.' Yes, Jesus and his Spirit work differently than anything I've ever known. He'll show me the difference. Demons played tricks with my mind, and Jesus will free me in his way and time. This is true. The Bible can be trusted."

I turned to Ephesians and read aloud the sections that described the armor of God and then prayed, "Lord, cover me with your armor. Come, Lord Jesus. I love you, Lord Jesus. Protect me through the night. Jesus, sweet Jesus, come," until the haranguing subsided. I then crawled back into bed, drew up my knees, clutched the Bible to my chest, and repeated the name of Jesus until his peace reigned within me and I fell asleep.

That Tuesday I met with David and Carrie and explained what had happened and what I did. "When free from these demons, will I be able to trust whatever comes into my mind?"

"No, the Bible tells us to test the spirits, for not everyone is from God, as you well know. But, yes, it will get easier."

"I wonder when my mind will clear. What door haven't I closed? What sin remains unconfessed? What ground have I given them that they still torment me so? Why are they still here?"

"I don't know," David replied warmly, "but I do know that God is in charge of this, and we're to listen to what he wants us to do. This morning while praying, these Scriptures came to mind, and I thought we could read them together. They come from Psalm 91. Verse 1 says, 'Whoever dwells in the shelter of the Most High will rest in the shadow of the Almighty' And further down, verse 5 says, 'You will not fear the terror of night, nor the arrow that flies by day,' This is a promise from God. We can count on this. No matter what, God is our refuge," David said, smiling at me.

I immediately lightened, and my fear vanished.

"Now I suggest we praise God," David said. "I've brought some hymns and song sheets. Together let us praise God." David began to sing the doxology, "Praise God from whom all blessings flow," and Carrie and I joined in. For the next half hour, we praised God for his majesty, faithfulness, and for sending his Son

Jesus. Then David read 1 John 4:4, "You, dear children, are from God and have overcome them, because the one who is in you is greater than the one who is in the world."

As we closed, David said, "Perhaps those specializing in the deliverance ministries could help you. Would you like for me to make some calls for you?"

"That would be fine. I'm willing to try anything."

The pastors moved through the rows of people stacked three deep around the stage, speaking in low tones, placing a hand on a head, putting an arm on a shoulder, and praying.

Some of those prayed for cried silently, others sobbed and then smiled. Friends and prayer ministers wrapped an arm around a waist, held tight, and prayed also for forgiveness, healing, provision, strength. I sat sideways on a folding chair watching them move, waiting my turn. The praise team swayed and sang softly in the background, and the demons taunted mercilessly.

The crowd thinned, and a pastor approached. "You must be Sharon. Your pastor said that you would be here tonight. We'll meet in the back room."

Once in the office, I sat on the folding chair across from him, and a female prayer minister stood behind him, praying silently. After he prayed aloud, I gave him a short history and described my current situation. "Since accepting Christ, my life has changed dramatically. I manage okay day to day, and most people would not suspect that I battle like I do. But it is still a battle and one that frightens people if I talk about it. I have faith that Jesus will free me completely, though I do wonder if there's more I should do. The demons are with me constantly. Even when they are not directly harassing me, I sense their presence, and the struggle exhausts me."

"How do they affect you now?"

"One thing they try to do is isolate me. None of my friends are Christian, and I'm barely able to initiate relationships. The spirits flood me with terror or hatred whenever I approach someone. I override these feelings by assuring myself that they are not mine, and once I start talking, I'm more myself. Then as I leave, they bombard me with accusations, enumerating everything I did or said wrong. They also attack God, pastors, the church, and the Bible. I try to ignore these things. Their attacks seem to come in waves, and occasionally they leave me alone completely. It's clear they want to keep me isolated from others and not to trust God and Jesus Christ as the way to him."

"It must be very hard on you."

"Yes, and I'm grateful that you understand and believe me when I say that these demons are not me! Really, I'm a much different person than how I appear when under their influence. But I don't know what to do to make them go away. I'm pretty much at a loss."

"Do you know how many are with you now?"

"No, I really don't because they lie. I thought I channeled five spirits, but now I don't know. It could have been just one or two taking on various personalities. The Bible says that they only know to lie, there is no truth in them, and that has been my experience. I no longer talk to them or acknowledge their presence. I have a strong sense of who I am separate from them, but I just can't be myself. Do you understand?"

"Yes, I do understand, and tonight we will pray and ask God to reveal the sin or ground that gives them license to harass you. I will then ask you to confess the sin and I'll cast out the demon by the authority of Jesus Christ."

"I really don't know the ground. I've confessed every sin I'm aware of."

"Well, sometimes these things are discerned spiritually. God reveals to us the nature of the sins, and we then cast the demons out. You see, demons must submit to the authority of Jesus Christ."

"Do you want me to put any restraints on what the demons say or do? They get pretty vile you know."

"No. Just let me deal with it," he said and began praying. I complied, retreated, and meditated, using the techniques I employed when channeling. A demon spewed hatred throughout me and squared off against the pastor.

Using my voice and body, he hissed, "You can make me do nothing! Just try. I'll show you who she belongs to."

"In the name of Jesus Christ be quiet."

The demon sneered, leaned forward, and taunted, "I'll do whatever, whenever I please."

"You are a defeated foe. Now tell me what is your name?"

"Little Red Riding Hood," he said, "and you better watch out or the big bad wolf will eat you up." He laughed sinisterly and added, "Now leave me alone. She's mine."

The pastor stood and said authoritatively, "You demon of witchcraft, in the name of Jesus Christ, I say be gone. Jesus is Lord, and you must submit to his authority."

The demon spat at him, and I broke in, "I'm sorry. I didn't know he would do that. I'm so sorry. Do you want me to let him continue?"

"No. Sharon, are you aware of any occult activity that you haven't confessed?"

"No."

"Well, would you confess the sin of witchcraft?"

Though I had confessed this sin twice before, I said, Yes, of course." I prayed, "Lord, forgive me my sin of witchcraft, for I know that all divination is an abomination to you."

"Now, I'd like to talk to the demon again."

I complied, and he said, "Demon of witchcraft, I command you, by the authority of Jesus Christ, to leave this woman."

Filled with venom, the demon sneered, "She's not going to let me spit. What a shame," and I restrained the demon from physically lashing out at the pastor and assumed control of my body.

"I'm back. I didn't want him to hurt you."

"What did you feel as I was praying?"

"Well, as I watched, I'd say relief. That is how he is, and I feel some relief in knowing that you know about it. Sometimes I wonder if Christians really comprehend what Jesus saved us from. But, no, as you prayed, he did not relent. If the Bible says that he is obligated to submit to Jesus, and he doesn't, does that mean that I've not confessed something I should?"

"I don't know, Sharon, but I would assume that we have not discovered the ground for this demon. The Bible says that some demons will leave only by prayer and fasting. So I suggest that we set another appointment, and in the meantime, I'll ask some people to pray and fast for you, and we'll see where God wants us to go from here."

"It feels wretched to allow him to speak through me—he's so evil—but if I have to do this to get free, I'm willing. But I never want to speak to him myself. I do best when I focus on Jesus, fill my mind with Scriptures, and praise God. If I address him, I crumble under his deluge and he has a heyday."

"Then rely on us to do that for you, and you continue as you have. Are you involved in a church?"

"Yes, I attend two services Sunday morning, come here Sunday night, and I'm involved in a Bible study and prayer group during the week. My primary mission right now is to understand what it means to be a Christian." I laughed and added, "Really, if I could bring a bedroll and sleep in church I would. It's where I feel the safest."

"Yes, I understand. Well, take heart; they do have to go, and we'll be praying, interceding for you. Tonight when praying for you, I had a vision. I saw you falling into a dark hole and landing on a cross. There you stood, your feet firmly planted on the cross, suspended in darkness. Then a feeling of strength came over me, and I sensed that the Lord was telling you that he has secured you and will lift you out of darkness."

"That's exactly what I believe and what I know to be happening."

"Well, please call me, and we'll set an appointment for next week."

"I will, and thank you for your help." I opened the office door and entered the worship center, where I heard laughter and saw the musicians folding music stands, men stacking chairs, and children playing tag around women picking up scraps of paper from the floor.

In my car I prayed, "Dear Lord, I'm a soldier in your army, but I don't know what I should do. Jesus, what would you have me do? I will do as they say, but please, Lord, correct me if what I do is not in accordance with your will. Thank you, Lord, for these people. Bless them, Lord. I'm so grateful they understand."

But something gnawed at me.

# CHAPTER 15

# Stand with Jesus

*Be alert and of sober mind. Your enemy the devil prowls around like a roaring lion looking for someone to devour. Resist him, standing firm in the faith* (1 Pet. 5:8–9).

*Standing with Jesus seemed too simple, but Jesus showed me that standing, loving and obeying him was exactly what he wanted me to do. He would remove demons in His time and way.*

SINCE SATAN HAD DESIGNED AN elaborate counterfeit and organized an army of demons to implement it for the sole purpose of confounding people's relationships with God and themselves, I concluded that the real thing must be incredible! But because those in the healing and deliverance ministries used methods similar to those I had learned at the spiritualist church, I privately wondered how they differentiated the real thing from the counterfeit.

For instance, after the pastor confronted the demon harassing me, he received a vision of me standing on a cross and automatically accepted it as one from the Lord Jesus. Why? Was it because the symbols were Christian ones and the message hopeful and in agreement with Scripture?

Because he spoke authoritatively, I gave him the benefit of the doubt and assumed that the place in his mind where visions appeared was protected from Satan's influence. Satan could not deceive him as he did me, and I tentatively concluded that only those coming out of the occult need worry about such things.

The issue was an important one for me, because I now put myself under the authority of those specializing in the deliverance ministries, and in addition to the Bible and prayer, they based their counsel on what they received from visions and special revelation. I followed their counsel, that is, confessed a particular sin or repeated a Scripture as they spiritually discerned the need for me to do so. I did what they said but privately questioned the wisdom of automatically trusting whatever came to mind no matter how wise, beautiful, or seemingly appropriate. Did they know how well Satan deceives? I knew firsthand that Satan could replicate sensations of strength, beauty, peace, love, and joy when masquerading as an angel of light, and all the while destroying my soul. Even now he influenced my intuition, present perceptions, memories, feelings, thoughts, and body. When I was in the occult and acting as a channel, the demon spirits conveyed their messages by impressing pictures in my mind, sensations in my body, and a sensing as in an intuited revelation. Often the person receiving the information felt encouraged, and furthermore, what I said often resonated with something they already sensed to be true. My ability to convey information about which I had no prior knowledge, the helpfulness of the message, and their understanding of its underlying significance confirmed that I had successfully served as a clear channel for spirit communication.

For example, one night during class at the spiritualist church, when I sat quietly staring at the black expanse before me, twinkling stars appeared, followed by a ball of light expanding and brightening the heavens. Quickly it disappeared, replaced by a red flower surrounded by lush green grass. A woman's hand picked and pushed the flower forward as if handing it to me, and my heart warmed, filled with love. Then I heard, "Tell Joan to open her heart and that her friend needs her now." In the vision, light refracted through raindrops and cast a rainbow on a window pane.

My body filled with awe, ecstasy. Suddenly the black expanse returned. The spirit girl, our teacher and guide, moved from person to person around the circle, talking with one and then another as each reported what he or she saw. Each one offered an interpretation, which she then corrected or corroborated. I often sat for a half hour or more waiting my turn, meditating and reviewing the images in my mind. Then she said, "And, Sharon, what did you see, hear, or feel?"

"First I saw black as if the universe, some stars, and then the light. Next I saw a flower, a red one, surrounded by green grass, which a hand picked and gave to me. I heard that Joan is to open her heart and that her friend needs her now."

She broke in to say, "Very good, Sharon. What color red did you see?"

"It was a warm, rich color, and a feeling of love engulfed me."

"Yes, and that shade of red symbolizes an open, loving heart. Was the green vibrant?"

"Yes, and I assumed that to be a symbol of growth."

"Yes, it is. Your guides are telling me that you are receiving their communications very well. Joan's friend is in trouble and needs a special hand now. You're becoming very sensitive to their communications, but they would like to work a bit longer with you, so open your mind again. They have more to say. I'll come back to you when I complete the circle." I cleared my mind again and overheard Joan describe her friend's dilemma. Indeed, her friend had cried during a recent conversation. The spirit girl counseled Joan that her friend needed her and predicted that Joan would grow spiritually as she helped her.

From then on Joan assumed that I had revelatory information about her and sought my counsel. I depended on the spirit girl in a similar way and eventually trusted her counsel and perspective above my own on the most mundane matters such as my perceptions of people and situations, what to buy, and which studies to pursue. Rather than empower me, her help fostered a dependency that twisted into an obsession, the same as in Joan's relationship with me.

Now a similar dynamic occurred between those in the deliverance ministry and me, that is, I depended on them in much the same way I had Donna, the spirit girl she channeled, and my guides. Because the spirits continued to harass me, and I didn't know why, I believed that the cause must be spiritually discerned and remedied by them as they prayed. I attended many deliverance sessions, and although the content varied, they followed a pattern.

First the deliverance people listened as I described my situation. Then they read passages from the Bible pertinent to my dilemma. They asked God to cover us with the blood of Jesus and to direct our time of prayer. Then they invited the Holy Spirit to manifest, prompting them to pray in tongues, described as a special prayer language of the Holy Spirit. Next they asked the demon to manifest, and after he did, they interviewed him. During the conversation they spiritually discerned, through visions, sensations, direct voice, or intuition, the name of the spirit and its legal ground for harassing me. From this information they determined the nature of the sin that gave the spirit the right to bother me. I then confessed that sin and repeated aloud the truth of Scripture. Finally they called the demon back and commanded it to leave me.

After a couple of years of deliverance sessions and one particularly painful one, I stopped going. At this particular session, I explained to the counselor that Jesus Christ had set me free but that I continued to be spiritually harassed. I sat in a folding chair in his office as he called up every spirit I had ever channeled or spoken to. I watched them one by one coyly respond to his questions and authoritative use of Scripture. For an hour he systematically refuted their claims and then asked to talk to me.

"Are you saved?" he asked.

I had not heard the word saved used like that in the Episcopal Church, and so it confused me. "What do you mean?"

Alarmed, he turned to the woman who had accompanied me, "Well, is she?" he challenged.

"Yes, I think so. Yes, I'm sure of it."

I turned to my friend: "What does that mean—saved?"

"He's asking if you have accepted Jesus Christ as Lord and Savior."

Incredulous, I turned back to him and said firmly, "Jesus is my Lord and Savior." But the look on his face said he was not convinced, and I realized that since he had primarily talked to demons, he knew more about them than he knew about me.

Once in my car I counseled myself out loud, "I never remember Jesus interviewing and arguing with demons. Mostly he told them to leave, and sometimes he delivered people without ever addressing the demon. Why am I putting myself through this? I'm convinced that my faith in Jesus is enough! Period. Demons only know to lie. Why believe anything they say? I must call David."

For the last couple of years, whenever I reached the outer limit of my understanding of Scripture, I turned to David Stark. We averaged an hour-long meeting every three months, during which I poured out my thoughts and he helped me evaluate them in light of Scripture. That day we met at a restaurant.

After we greeted each other and prayed, I pulled out a folder where I had listed my concerns and supporting verses from the Bible, organized into two columns headed "Pros" and "Cons."

"David, I'm struggling with an issue."

"First tell me how you're doing."

"Oh, my life's going well. I recently joined Cherry Hills Community Church, an Evangelical Presbyterian Church. Originally, I joined because I wanted Michael, who's now thirteen, to be a part of their youth program. He's happy there, and I'm absorbing the teaching like a sponge. People around me are coming to know Christ, and I'm excited when they do.

"I'm sleeping through the night most of the time, and my mind is more my own than not, although I sense the presence of spirits. I make better decisions. And I lead a simple life. I go to Michael's football games, where I'm team mom, work, and go to church Sunday mornings and once during the week. I also pray with others and continue to pray, write in my journal, and read the Bible for an hour each morning. I'd say that's my mainstay. Really I'm much better!"

"Sounds good. I'm amazed at the transformation in you. You're a different woman than the person who walked into my office a couple years ago."

"Yes. And I feel it on the inside too."

"Wonderful! What's the issue?"

"Well, the demons are still with me, and specifically, I wonder what Jesus expects of me. I'm beginning to think that deliverance is more a process than an event and that my faith in him is the key ingredient."

"Yes, but what puts you in conflict with that?"

"Well, I get confused. Those in the deliverance ministry say the demons must be confronted directly and cast out before they will leave. When I go to the deliverance people for prayer, I do sense the Holy Spirit, but then afterward the harassment continues, and I think I've somehow failed, like I'm not the Christian I should be or that I'm damaged goods beyond repair or some such nonsense. What I appreciate most about the way they pray is their faith in the victory of Christ over evil. That genuinely consoles me, but sometimes I feel desperate to find the right person to pray for me, as if only a certain person can free me. That can't be right!"

"I didn't realize you were doing this. It sounds like it has been hard."

"Yes, it has. Also, I'm aware that sometimes I treat prayer as if it's magic, believing that if I pray right, certain things will happen. I remind myself to put my faith in Jesus, not in my ability to pray, but that gets confusing given where I've come from. And finally, I find the sessions humiliating. I hate allowing demons the use of my body, simply hate it!" Tears welled, and I fumbled for the napkin.

"Sharon, then stop. Don't do it anymore." David reached for his Bible and read, "Be alert and of sober mind. Your enemy the devil prowls around like a roaring lion looking for someone to devour. Resist him, standing firm in the faith. . . . And the God of all grace, who called you to his eternal glory in Christ, after you have suffered a little while, will himself restore you and make you strong, firm and steadfast. To him be the power for ever and ever. Amen." (1 Pet. 5:6–9a, 10–11).

David handed me the Bible, and after I read the passage, he said, "This is his promise to us."

I said, "Yes, I believe this. It's not for me to say how God delivers others, but I really sense he wants me to simply trust him to lead me out of this. Talking with demons seems unnecessary."

"Is there more?"

"Yes, I get worried when Christians automatically assume that every vision, revelatory dream, and inspiration is from God, and it's particularly difficult when the message is for me. I believe the Holy Spirit speaks to us, but I wish people would be more cautious. When I'm reading the Bible or praying and God directs me toward a particular thing, I have to sit with it a while. I pray, talk with friends, and read the Bible. Eventually I'm sure of what God wants, but sometimes it takes a while, and usually he speaks softly."

"Yes, I know what you mean, and he works that way with me. Is there more?"

"Yes, sometimes I dissect my life, searching for any sin that might give the demons permission to hang around, like I have to be perfect—confess every sin before they'll stop beating me up!"

David again leafed through the Bible, "Yes, here it is: 'A man is not justified by observing the law, but by faith in Jesus Christ. So we, too, have put our faith in Christ Jesus that we may be justified by faith in Christ and not by observing the law, because by observing the law no one will be justified' (Gal. 2:16).

"Jesus Christ is the perfect One. He alone is a perfect fulfillment of the law. God knew that we could never be righteous while separated from him, so he sent his Son to be our righteousness, and we are now justified because of what he did. It's a miracle, really."

"Yes. I think it's time I stop scrambling around trying to figure out why these demons won't leave. I'm much better when I keep my eyes on Christ and know that I'm in him." I added, "I've pleaded with God to take this away; and it confuses me when he doesn't."

David said, "Well, you know, Paul related a similar dilemma. He pleaded with God to remove a thorn from his flesh, as he called it, but Jesus answered, 'My grace is sufficient for you, for my power is made perfect in weakness'" (2 Cor. 12:9).

I smiled, "That passage always comforts me."

"And it does many Christians. Continue seeking him as you have been. He's taking good care of you."

"Yes, he is. When demons assault me, and I cling to God, it is then that I know him best. That's a sad state of affairs, isn't it—that it's when I'm incapacitated that I draw close to God!"

"Yes, but we all have the same struggle, and that is why we desperately need God's grace." David shifted forward and said, "Sharon, let's pray."

Jesus Christ delivered me—just not how I originally expected. Rather than a sudden relief, as when someone says the right word and demons flee, the demons simply faded from my awareness as my relationship with God deepened. I fixed my gaze on God, obeyed him, and he changed me from the inside out. The demons lost their hold as others prayerfully interceded for me and as I applied God's Word to my life, prayed, worshiped, read the Bible, helped others, and walked by faith.

But it was a struggle. Daily I strained to differentiate what was of God or Satan or me. I asked God to speak to me through his Word rather than through visions, intuitions, and physical sensations, and I abdicated all experience to the authority of the Holy Bible. I read, "But when he, the Spirit of truth, comes, he will guide you into all truth. . . . He will bring glory to me by taking from what is mine and making it known to you. All that belongs to the Father is mine" (John 16:13–15). I applied God's truth to all aspects of my life and trusted that God would make his truth known to me and quell the battle in his time and way.

I reminded myself that hateful feelings were not of God, and I denied expressions of terror, rage, and various forms of lust, envy, and greed. I recited Scripture verses, which I typed on small cards and carried with me to remind me of what was true. I trusted that as I meditated on these things that God would conform me to the image of his Son, Jesus Christ. I took this promise of his literally as I engaged in the warfare.

For instance, after a Sunday morning service, the pastor approached, extended his hand, and said, "Welcome to our church. I understand that you were involved in the New Age. Were you in it long?"

"Yes, about eleven years."

"It's hard for me to understand how people believe that stuff."

Instantly a mixture of terror and shame overwhelmed me, and I scrambled for a response. "I don't know," I mumbled and excused myself. My insides shook as demons infused me with adrenaline; terror transformed to rage at the pastor. Then, when I was almost out the door, shame engulfed me, similar to how the abused feels toward an abuser. I somehow deserved punishment for being stupid and gullible. As I approached my car, I became very fearful.

"This is not of God or me. None of it," I said aloud. Once in my car, I fumbled through my purse for my stack of Scripture cards and found 2 Timothy 1:7 and read aloud, "God did not give us a spirit of timidity, but a spirit of power, of love and of self-discipline." I repeated it and then prayed, "Lord, I pray that you create me anew with your Spirit. Remove this fear and shame."

By the time I reached home, I had calmed. As I got out of the car, I prayed, "Lord, I forgive him. He had no way of knowing."

At other times a response transformed to an obsession, as when I tipped over a glass of water at a church dinner and apologized as I wiped it up. The scene replayed in my mind for the next twenty minutes. Then I prayed, "Lord, I know that you gave me a spirit of love and self-control, and, Father, I take every thought captive and make it obedient to you. Thank you, Lord Jesus." My mind quieted.

I also claimed that promise when I trembled at the thought of meeting people as I approached the church on Sunday mornings. As I walked in by faith, Jesus faithfully sustained me with his Spirit, and he healed me.

Now I understood that I could never heal myself: My Creator had made me, and he alone could transform me. As Jesus changed me, the demons lost their hold, not by a dramatic departure, but a slipping away. Jesus did this as I embraced him and took my position as a full-fledged member of his kingdom, tending the fruit of his Spirit growing in me.

# CHAPTER 16

# God Redeemed My Life

*"Praise be to the Lord, the God of Israel, because he has come to his people and redeemed them* (Luke 1:68).

*The attacks gradually lessened as I joined the church and served Christ. I loved the Savior!*

I MARVELED AT THE CHANGES in my life. At Christmastime only four years ago I had stared at a white ceramic cherub hanging beneath the angel on the tree, wondering where to put my faith and unable to prepare a meal, complete a thought, or make a living without the permission of malevolent forces. Now my life was different. I had a Christian counseling practice, a new house and new friends, and God's presence in our home. Yes, I thanked Jesus this Christmas.

I centered the seven-foot Colorado pine in front of the partition separating the living room from the kitchen. The white wallpaper, textured in swirls, created a soft backdrop for the silvery-green branches cascading down the trunk. Flames lapped the compressed log in the free-standing fire place, reminiscent of the one I had when living in the mountains. The fire warmed the living room and emitted a soft glow that was reflected in translucent bulbs, white ceramic angels, and sprinkles of tinsel adorning the tree.

This indigenous pine had a reputation for enduring in dry climates and painted a pretty picture close to the fire place, but within three days, while pouring water into the stand, I noticed that the silver-tipped branches were quite brown beneath the lights and glitter. So Michael and I stripped it, loaded it into the trunk of my Honda, and returned it to the lot. The owner fondly identified it as a golden pine, a euphemism for dead.

Four years ago, I could not have weathered an incident such as this, but now we simply bought another and placed it near the piano at the other end of the room where Michael practiced as I prepared breakfast in the mornings. Positioned on the corner, between the kitchen and living room, we could see it from the table as well as from most rooms on the main level of the small ranch house.

"What do you want to eat this morning, Michael?"

He stopped his playing and hollered, "Quesadillas!" as if I were downstairs instead of standing in the kitchen ten feet from the piano on the other side of the partition.

"For breakfast?" I screamed back.

Enjoying the repartee, he retorted, "Oh, Mom, I'm right here; you don't have to yell!"

"Right, and you still have ten minutes left on your practicing," I laughed. Yes, laughter and order had returned to our home.

While rinsing the skillet and spatula, I glanced out the window down the tree-lined street over the shingled roofs at the mountains peeking through bare trees, and smiled. A soft winter haze blurred the Rockies, but my heart leaped all the same. "Beautiful." I briefly reflected on times past when I thought their energy empowered me and said, "Majestic creations of God!

They're God's creation, just like me." Smiling, I returned to the stove and plopped the folded tortillas in the greased skillet and covered it with a lid.

I opened the refrigerator door and spotted the meatloaf leftover from the night before. "Hey, there's my lunch!" I hauled it, along with mayo and whole wheat bread to the counter across from the refrigerator. Then I returned to the opened door and put the milk and orange juice on the table and said to Michael, "Breakfast is almost served, so finish up." My mind kept step with this chock-full, busy morning.

My mind no longer betrayed me nor prevented me from performing my responsibilities. I retrieved my Bible from the chair across from the tree where I spent my early morning time with the Lord, sat down at the table, and opened it to Luke. Michael joined me at the table, and we read a portion of the Christmas story. Then we prayed, thanking God for his glorious gift, Jesus Christ.

Midway through breakfast, Michael's friend Scott arrived, and while they did whatever thirteen-year-olds do when out of adult hearing and seeing, I made my lunch, loaded the dishwasher, and stuffed reports into my briefcase. The high school wrestling coach resided across the street, next to a coach from another suburban high school; and two doors down, on our side of the street, lived the head football coach from the high school where Michael would attend next year. As a single mother, I liked being encircled by these bastions of authority and smiled as the two adolescent boys lowered their heads while walking past their houses to middle school, six blocks away. God provided well for us.

I enjoyed Michael's friends and only occasionally embarrassed him, as when I asked a friend if she thought the quartz crystal dangling from her neck had special powers or if she wore it because she thought it was pretty. "Oh, it's just a pretty stone," she answered, "but I know some kids at school who think it gives them special power. I say that's weird!" Or when I asked another if he knew Jesus Christ. "No, not really," he said, "but I've been to church," and he told me about the service.

More often I sought opportunities to speak openly about what God had done in my life. After a Sunday service, I approached a visiting youth pastor from Boulder and said, "I was involved in the New Age for many years and spent time in Boulder while getting a doctorate. If you'd like, I'd be happy to present my testimony to the kids in your youth program. I've not done this before, but I'd like to try." He nodded enthusiastically and called the following week to schedule a talk with their Monday night youth group.

Petrified, I immediately called a friend and asked her to pray for me. "Please intercede for me, Rebecca. I haven't a clue what I'm going to say."

"Of course, I will, and I'll talk to Ron about the two of us driving you there. I'd love to help."

Buoyed by praise music and reassuring smiles from Rebecca, I relaxed in the backseat as Ron drove us to a large ranch house in the Boulder suburbs. The din grew louder as we walked the sandstone path leading to the house, and when I opened the front door, my confidence vanished—music blared, girls giggled, boys yelled from one room to another, and clumps of teenagers sprawled and conversed in hushed tones. I mentally grabbed a Bible verse that Rebecca and I had prayed the week before: "I will go before you and will level the mountains]; I will break down gates of bronze and cut through bars of iron" (Isa. 45:2). I reminded myself that God, not me, prepared their hearts to hear what I had to say.

Still my hands and mind numbed as we moved through the teeming teens to find Pastor Steve conversing with two boys in the kitchen. He smiled broadly and said, "Welcome, Sharon. We'll get started in five minutes, so help yourself to something to drink." He gestured to a table filled with pop and potato chips, and added, "Good, you brought friends! Welcome," and he warmly shook Rebecca's and Ron's hand.

Soon Pastor Steve moved to the front of the beige-draped bay window, and the commotion and music stilled. The kids fanned around him squeezing three to a chair and six to a couch, leaning against knees, hanging over shoulders, slumping against walls, fidgeting, staring, and making faces at friends. Rebecca and Ron smiled and winked as they sat against the back wall, and after prayer and introductions, I stood to face the group.

"I'm here to present my testimony—my firsthand account of what Jesus Christ has done for me. I've made mistakes in my life, and the biggest one was losing faith in Jesus when I was about your age. I hope that by sharing my story you can avoid some of the pitfalls I fell into. I want to encourage you to remain steadfast in your faith and to trust Jesus with matters closest to your heart.

"I know that people in Boulder express their spiritual beliefs in a variety of ways. Christians attend church, Buddhists meditate, those following Native American traditions form medicine circles, and many others engage in various New Age practices. They meditate, worship nature, study the stars, and profess to heal the body by manipulating energy fields.

"Have you ever been curious about these practices? How many of you have been to a psychic or fortune-teller, played with a Ouija board, sought counsel from tarot cards, or played with a pendulum?" Some lifted a finger, raised a hand, or waved an arm. "Would you tell the rest of us what happened?" A very wide-eyed girl related how, while at a slumber party, she and two girlfriends played with a Ouija board. "The pointer moved by itself and spelled the name of a spirit. Then the spirit told us about his life on earth a hundred years ago."

"Sure, Melissa!" a boy chided.

"No, really, I didn't push the pointer. It moved by itself."

I interjected, "Did it scare you? Or perhaps make you curious?"

"Well, I was more scared than anything, but my friend really got into it."

"Anybody else had something happen to them?"

A boy related an experience he and a friend had when visiting a palm reader at the summer Renaissance Festival. Another girl described her mother's seance sessions held in their home.

"Many people think these games and activities are harmless, but they are dangerous. It's easy to get fascinated with this power, drawn deeper into it, until it becomes an obsession. You kind of lose track of yourself."

"Yeah, a friend of mine went to a psychic who told him of his past life as an Indian," a boy said, "and now he wears this cord around his neck with some weird thing attached." I smiled and said, "The Bible warns us to stay away from mediums and all forms of divination or fortune-telling. The source of the information is evil and can take over your life. That's what happened to me. I used to be a psychic and thought it was harmless, even helpful. But I was wrong, very wrong. When I tried to stop, I discovered that the spirits, or demons, giving the information wanted to control and destroy me. They wouldn't leave. It was only when I confessed my sin and asked Jesus Christ to be my Lord and Savior that I was freed from their control.

"Now, I'm not saying that everyone who visits a medium, plays with a Ouija board, or reads tarot cards will be taken over by demons, but I am warning you that engaging in these activities opens the door to evil influences. As Christians we know that we can turn to our mighty warrior, Jesus Christ, who protects and provides all we need. If some of you haven't accepted Jesus as your Lord and Savior and want to, I'd be happy to pray with you when we close. Do you have questions?"

Hands shot up around the room, and for the next hour we shared stories and Scriptures. Pastor Steve closed the meeting with prayer and invited those desiring individual prayer to come forward.

Once invited, a girl named Jane left the wall and slipped around the edges of the group to stand by my side and tug at my sleeve. I took her hand, and we sat knee to knee in a corner. She said, "I played with a Ouija board and got weirded out. My mom is into the same things you were." She began to cry, "My dad became a Christian last year, and I want to be one too, but I'm scared."

"God tells us in the Bible that his perfect love pushes out fear, and that's been true in my life. When I look to God, his love fills my heart and the fear goes away. God loves you and your father and your mother."

"But I'm worried about my mom. She's going to be mad if I become a Christian. She's really mad at. Dad."

"Yes, I understand how difficult that can be. But once Jesus lives in your heart, you'll be able to love her more. God specializes in love and wants you to share it with others."

"Yes, this has happened to my dad. He's really changed. Okay. What do I need to do?"

"Well, first you confess to God that you have sinned against him. And mention anything that comes to your mind. Then ask him to forgive you."

Jane bowed her head and prayed aloud, "God, I have sinned against you. And I used the Ouija board, visited the psychic, played with tarot cards, and talked to spirits in my mind. Please forgive me."

"Good. Now ask Jesus to be Lord and Savior of your life."

"Oh, Jesus, forgive me." Her shoulders trembling, she cried, "Help me. Be my Lord and Savior. I'm sorry." After a minute, she grabbed a tissue, blew her nose, and beamed, "I did it!"

I hugged her and smiled, "Yes, you did! Welcome to God's kingdom. And thank you, Lord, for forgiving Jane of her sins and ushering her into your kingdom. Jane, what a wonderful decision you've made! Let's go tell Pastor Steve!"

Moments like these brought me joy, and the more I exercised my faith, the stronger it grew. Though sometimes I identified with Peter, who climbed out of his fishing boat to walk to Jesus on the Sea of Galilee. I too cried, "But, Jesus, I can't walk on water," and sank as I took my eyes off him. But always, whenever I grasped his hand, Jesus held me firm.

In May 1989 I attended a women's retreat sponsored by the women's ministry at Cherry Hills Community Church. I sat in a banquet hall in the upstairs of a castle at Glen Eyrie, a Christian conference center in Colorado Springs, listening to an attractive, dark-haired speaker describe how God used our brokenness to bring us closer to him. During the closing sessions she asked us to write a letter to Jesus, "In it I want you to tell him what's on your heart, and after you're finished, address the envelope and hand the letter to me. I'll mail them to you, and you should receive them next week."

She passed paper and envelopes down the rows, and I wondered, "What haven't I said?" Then I wrote:

*Dear Jesus,*

I want to thank you for saving me and leading me like you do. I love you with all my heart. But don't you think you were a bit hard on me? You knew that I was like a deer inside, and yet you allowed Satan to ravage me. Why? Why did I have to visit hell? Oh, Lord, I wish there could have been another way to, know you like I do now. I've never known such pain.

Lord, I don't understand, but I do trust you. I do. And I mean it when I say, "Not my will but yours be done" in my life. I'm sincere when I say, "Here am I, send me." Yes, I get afraid, but, Lord, more than anything, I pray that through your Spirit you conform me to your image and allow me to be your servant.

Thank you, Jesus. I look forward to seeing you in heaven.

*Love, Sharon*

I wiped my eyes and cheeks and surveyed the other tear-stained women who, with pads perched on knees, earnestly poured their hearts out to God. The leader looked beleaguered as she sipped her glass of water, and my heart warmed. I wanted to pray with her, so I closed my eyes and asked, "Lord, should I offer to do that?"

I rose from my chair and immediately sat back down. Flooded with embarrassment, I thought, You haven't spoken two words to her all weekend. Don't be presumptuous; she has plenty of people to pray with her.

I prayed, "Jesus, what would you have me do?" Feeling shy, I picked up my Bible and notebook, handed her my letter, and left the room to sit on the steps down the hall. Suddenly ensconced in a spiritual battle, my mind whirled: Yes, that was from God. No, it wasn't. Yes, you should pray. No, you shouldn't. I prayed, "Lord, you ask us to pray without ceasing, and Lord, I intercede for this woman. Refresh and protect her, Lord—both her and her family. Bless this ministry."

My hands covered my face as I prayed, and I sensed someone sit down near me. When I opened my eyes, I faced the back of the leader and silently prayed, "Lord, thank you." Then I said aloud to her, "Would you like for me to pray for you?"

"Oh, thank you. Yes, I would like that very much," she said. "Seven people came to the Lord this weekend, and I couldn't be happier, but I'm so tired. Yes, please pray for me, and then let's pray for these new believers in Christ. How gracious God is." I moved to her step and, sitting with her knee to knee, began to pray.

As I grew in knowledge of the Bible, I attended seminars offered by Christian pastors on divination. I entered the auditorium as the man was beginning his talk. Taking a seat at one end of a row of folding chairs, I saw him wave a deck of cards and perform a sleight-of-hand magic trick. His hands moved quickly, and the hundred or so people in the audience looked as baffled as I was by what he did. To expose his trickery, he repeated his act in slow motion, then said, "See how easily we're fooled? This I do for fun, but psychics play a more sinister game. They want you to believe they are communicating with spirits and have special gifts for predicting the future. In fact, like magicians, they are masters at creating illusions. They manipulate people by preying on vulnerability and appealing to a desire to know the future. Relying on their intuition, they read nonverbal communications, listen for responses, tell people what they want to hear, and take their money. It's a multi-million-dollar racket and as Christians we must be informed.

"It works like this. The medium says, 'I'm sensing a female presence? She is smiling at you.'" He paused and gave the audience a "give-me-a-break" look. "Come on. By the time we reach adulthood, most of us know a woman who has died." The audience chuckled, and he added, "Chances are at some point she smiled at you. Does someone like that come to mind?" Some in the audience nodded, "See? And what are we tempted to say, 'Oh, yes, that was Aunt Mildred.' . . . or whatever her name was. And what does the psychic say? 'Yes, that's who is here. I'm getting confirmation on that. She's telling me that you are doing well in *most* areas of your life. But you are struggling with something . . . Let see, is it your job? Possibly a relationship?' The psychic looks intently at your face and waits for you to confirm which it is. Then she says, 'Don't worry, the problem will resolve itself.'"

Shifting gears, he paused and said, "Don't we all have at least one problem? And don't we want reassurance that it will turn out okay? Think about it. . . . If we are to believe the psychics, those who consult them have rosier futures than all the other people on the planet." He waved his hand as if performing his magic trick and said, "Our problems are simply going to vanish without us taking any responsibility for them." He laughed with the audience. Shaking his head, he said, "What a power trip!"

My insides quivered, mostly from fear that if I spoke up he would call me a liar or manipulator. I wanted to say that it was quite possible for demons to influence a psychic as well as the person receiving the reading, no matter how inconsequential or uninformed the reading. While sitting there, I thought, "It's the power inspiring the practice that makes divination dangerous, and that can't be discerned by analyzing what is said or even by scrutinizing the character of the medium. It's better to assume that demons are always involved. Some psychics are scoundrels and some well-intended, but they are all influenced by demons to some degree."

I retreated to the restroom and, resting my hands on the sink, looked at myself in the mirror and whispered, "The way he mocks mediums, it would seem that going to a psychic is more foolish than dangerous and sinful. He underestimates the ability of demons to deceive people. What if something supernatural happens during the reading? What are the people to believe then? No, we are to stay away not because it's a waste of time and money, although that is true, but because evil inspires the practice and because God says so. But how many Christians believe this?" I could not say.

# CHAPTER 17

# The Love of Christ

*See what great love the Father has lavished on us, that we should be called children of God! And that is what we are! The reason the world does not know us is that it did not know him* (1 John 3:1).

*The Love of Christ was difficult to receive. It was simply too wonderful to be true. Surely, I must do something or be a certain way to be worthy of God's love. No, faith in Christ sufficed. Amazing grace. Amazing love.*

### Fall 1990

ONE NIGHT WHILE DRIVING HOME from a lecture, I stopped at church to attend a dance for singles held every Friday in the gymnasium. Muffled strains of "I love rock 'n' roll music" drifted through the cool Colorado night as I approached the people chatting in clusters on the steps and lawn.

Once in the gym, I warmed as if in a sauna and wormed through swarms of people to the edge of the dance floor where couples and singles of all ages and sizes jumped up and around with their hands over their heads, popping their fingers to tunes from the fifties, sixties, and seventies. The singles pastor, decked in a white tee-shirt and jeans, headset over his ears, lip-synched to the music while, close behind, our music minister moved to the beat and retrieved discs.

Sweat gathered in beads on my forehead and trickled down my sides underneath my black silk shirt and gray suit jacket as I weaved around bodies in a steady retreat to the wall next to the ice and pop. Sipping on a diet soda and feeling more fifteen than forty-eight, I smiled, swayed to the beat, and gave myself thirty minutes before bailing out.

The tempo changed, and the singer crooned, "Only you," and it dawned on me that while plastered against the wall, the likelihood of me dancing was slim, so I inched a layer closer to the floor. A blond-headed man dressed in a white shirt, pullover sweater, and suit pants approached and introduced himself as Bob. Then he asked, "Would you like to dance?"

"Yes, that would be nice."

Bob led me to the dance floor and asked, "I've seen you in church. Do you come to these dances often?"

"No, a couple times maybe. How about you?"

"Oh, off and on," he said and gently guided me around the floor.

His head eight inches above mine and arm circling my back, I quivered like a school girl and was both relieved and saddened when the song ended. I wiped my palms on my skirt, stepped back to look him full in the face, and said in my grown-up voice, "Thank you. That was very nice."

"Would you like to dance another?" I nodded, and we did, and then Bob said, "Thank you very much" and left. So did I.

While driving home I tried to imagine how I would explain to an everyday kind of person the events of my life, "For ten or so years demons harassed me, and in the spring of 1987 Jesus Christ set me free. God is making me over, and I estimate that socially and emotionally I'm a teenager. What have you been up to?" I shook my head. "Another leap in faith!"

A month and a half later I attended another dance, and Bob approached, and we danced two songs. He stopped me as I went out the door, "Would it be okay if I called you? Perhaps we could go to lunch?"

"Yes, that would be nice," I smiled. Then I retrieved my business card from my purse, wrote my home phone number on the back, and said, "You can call me here."

"Good, talk to you this week."

"Bye."

The following week we met for lunch, and two weeks later for breakfast. We ordered, talked of business and church, and when the food arrived, he reached for my hand and prayed, asking God to bless our meal and time together. My heart stirred, and I thought, "He loves God as much as I do." I looked into his deep brown eyes and then concentrated on my food.

Whether my trembling reflected a fear of loving Bob or not being loved in return, I could not say, but I knew I had entered dangerous waters. The following year, as I prepared to marry Bob, God revealed one source of my fear.

### June 1991

My body conformed to the contour of the dark mahogany pew as I sat on the aisle toward the back of the church waiting for Dr. Neil Anderson to begin his weeklong conference in Topeka, Kansas. "What a lovely church!" I thought, noting the dark hardwood floors, polished mahogany railing traversing the altar, red carpeted steps, and gilded, opened Bible next to a plain gold cross.

Like most young lovers, in my passion for Christ, I sometimes perceived mine to be the truest love, as if no one before or after could have such an experience, but here in this church I sensed that generations of lovers preceded me. Here people had prayed, devoured Scripture, and loved their neighbors. Although I knew none of the five hundred attending, I remembered what Paul wrote to the church in Ephesus, "Consequently, you are no longer foreigners and strangers, but fellow citizens with God's people and also members of his household, built on the foundation of the apostles and prophets, with Christ Jesus himself as the chief cornerstone" (Eph. 2:19—20). Certainly, I felt it in this place. For five days Neil Anderson used passages from the Bible, lectures, cartoons, anecdotes, and testimonies as evidence for my position in Christ. "Do you know who you are? You are a child of God, Christ's friend, a new creation, chosen of God and dearly loved." He hesitated and said, "Try to grasp how wide and long and high and deep is the love of Christ for you." I can't fathom love that wide, deep, long, and high, but I want to. I pondered, "Why do I resist my Father's love?" I thought of my natural father.

## 1958

Sunday nights, after washing the dishes and wiping the counters, my father and I retreated to play Ping Pong in the basement. Alternating sides to compensate for poor lighting, we assumed our position at our respective stations and prepared for battle. Because of his protruding stomach, he stood three feet from the table and hit the ball with cutting, hard swings, hurling the ball with dizzying speed. By the time I was sixteen, we were evenly matched and played fiercely though without malice.

Whenever I inched ahead, he broke stride, "Get ready! That's where it's coming," and he pointed to the table's edge. "Ready?"

With an impish grin and exaggerated backswing, he stopped midair, set the ball and paddle on the table, pulled at his belt, tucked in his shirt, sipped his tea, and said, "Sure gets hot!" Then he wiped his dry brow.

I remained poised and ready through most of the charade, but the way he wiped his forehead, as if cooking over a hot stove in August heat, tickled me, and I laughed. When I did, he wound up with lightning speed, and the ball ticked the edge on my side. I lunged, hit the wall, and wailed, "Dad, that's not fair!"

"How else am I going to win this game? I've taught you too well! Your serve," he smirked. Once ahead, he showed no mercy, but then neither did I.

I smacked the ball, causing it to catch the net and tumble to his side. With his mouth agape and eyes widened, he followed the dribbling ball till it rested against his belly. In mock despair, he flung his paddle to the ground, and I collapsed on the floor in hysterics.

This was our time—intense, fun, exhilarating. He left the next day and returned in a week or two to resume our play. I never bothered him with everyday concerns, and I consoled myself by saying that if my life were threatened, he would be there for me.

Four years later and ten years after his first heart attack, my father called me at college, "Your mom's gone this weekend, and I sure would like some company. How about coming home for the weekend?"

Concealing my frustration, I said, "Of course. I'll be home tomorrow night, Dad." I canceled my plans and drove three hundred miles home.

Sunday midday, eager to return to school, my car loaded and gassed, I hugged him and waved good-bye from the car. Clad in a brown, wool plaid shirt tucked into loose-fitting trousers secured with a brown leather belt around his broad girth, he stood in the doorway enduring the cold for a final good-bye. A sharp gust caught grayish strands of hair and fluttered them over his bald top. His face looked sad. He waved. What did it say—"Go, I'm fine. Have a wonderful life. I love you," or "Please don't go. I'm afraid. I'm home alone"? Probably both.

I smiled and left. Five days later my dad died.

My earthly father loved me dearly but left me to fend for myself, and I thought I loved him best by not complaining, by doing well, and by enjoying him when we were together. I naturally assumed that my heavenly Father loved in the same way: God desired my praise, prayers, service, and study of his Word, but now that I was off the precipice and anchored in faith, he expected me to fend for myself as he went about his business. But Neil Anderson said that I was God's business. I thought of my son. "I love Michael and want to be with him when he is weak or strong, a success or failure, in need or not. If I love that way, then how much more must God love me!"

Spontaneously I began talking to God, "Lord, I know you love me and want me close, but I have a hard time staying there with you. It feels strange to cling like a child yet be an adult. Nevertheless, you say it's the only way I can please you. "Why didn't my father trust you, Lord? I know he loved you, but he clung to his wife and children instead; and like Neil said, I reaped the consequence of Dad's sin and believed the lie that I must fend for myself.

"Then who of us is perfect? None. Didn't I put my own son at risk by chasing false prophets and gods? And you loved me and forgave me then, and so did Michael." I then prayed, "How great is the love you have lavished on me that I should be called your child! And that is what I am! Indeed!" (1 John 3:1). A weight lifted, and I sighed.

I returned my attention to Neil Anderson as he said, "Do you know that you are in Christ? You are free indeed!"

Yes, I am, I thought, and only from here can I truly love my neighbor and a husband!

God kept me close to himself as I developed a loving relationship with Bob as well as with other believers. I recalled as a teenager leaving Jesus to search for flesh and blood saviors, and now, thirty-some years later, I found the arms Christ used.

They included the ones who weekly sang, prayed, taught about the Bible, and spoke about God, and as my life joined with theirs, the Holy Spirit loved, sustained, and fulfilled his promise to complete the work he started in me. Not in one Sunday or even a year of Sundays was this accomplished, but through the years as I committed to learn about, worship, and serve God with other believers.

My church was large, and I attended Sunday mornings and Wednesday evenings. The pews fanned around the stage area and held approximately seventeen hundred people. When sitting there, my eyes riveted on the cross sculpted into the wall behind the stage. It consisted of concentric crosses graduating in size with the smallest in the center, expanding until they dominated the wall. Week after week, year after year, I looked at that awesome, somber reminder of the price Jesus paid to secure my heart. Yes, the beauty of the cross drew me to this church.

But then so did the music and the prayer. Together we praised God and prayed for the sick, the abandoned, and the less fortunate, as well as our church, city, country, and special situations in the world. The teaching and preaching also drew me. On Wednesday nights our teaching pastor expounded on the Old and New Testaments, describing the people and events of biblical times. He talked about God and his plans and purpose for our life. The Bible came alive as we studied the books of the Bible, life of Christ, and work of the apostles. He took God very seriously, but not himself, and sometimes he teased and said, "You know we're all bozos on the bus." We laughed because we knew how desperately we needed God simply to function day to day.

Sunday after Sunday, year after year, our pastor bowed his head and prayed, "May these words of my mouth and this meditation of my heart be pleasing in your sight, LORD, my Rock and my Redeemer" (Ps 19:14). Then he picked up the Bible and said, "The Bible says. . . " He told us about God's character, about Jesus' work on our behalf, about the wiles of the Evil One, and about our commitment as a church to help the poor and tell others about Christ as well as to love and serve one another. "This is what it means to live a normal Christian life," he said, and I believed him because what he said agreed with the Bible and the Holy Spirit in me.

# CHAPTER 18

# Rescued and Redeemed!

*For he has rescued us from the dominion of darkness and brought us into the kingdom of the Son he loves, in whom we have redemption, the forgiveness of sins* (Col. 1:13–14).

*My ministry centered on sharing the gospel and talking about the enemy's tactics. I expected those who didn't know Christ to reject Satan's existence and capabilities, but I was surprised when many Christians also discounted his relevancy in everyday life.*

### Winter 1992

"YOU SEE, I HAVE A LEO rising, and center stage is my natural habitat," Amy said as she tossed her shoulder-length auburn hair and leveled her gaze at me.

Sensing she trusted me, I gently chided, "So, is this a permanent condition?"

Amy smiled, her dark green eyes issuing a discordant collage of sincerity, defiance, and vulnerability. She had originally sought my counsel concerning a difficulty in a personal relationship, but today she discussed her spiritual journey, described as "a heartfelt pursuance of truth." She assumed that as a Christian counselor I too was a spiritual sojourner, following the traditions of Jesus

Christ, a spiritual presence equal to Buddha and other ascended masters.

"Are you familiar with astrology?" she asked. I nodded.

"Well, then you know where this tendency of mine comes from. I need attention! Seems pretty basic to me!"

"I see. Who told you these things?"

"My astrologer. I met her in Santa Fe when I was with friends I met through est—you know, the Werner Erhard's seminars. I consult a lot of psychics, but this astrologer is the best."

"Why do you seek her counsel, Amy?"

Her face softened, and she said, "I want to know if I'll be okay, that is, if my life will turn out. It seems that no matter what I do or how hard I try, nothing works, and inevitably she puts her finger smack dab on the source of the problem. Amazing how she does that!"

"Yes, it's uncanny. How did you get interested in the supernatural?"

"In the early 1980s I went to a therapist specializing in rebirthing."

"What happened?"

"She had me lie on a mat, close my eyes, and breathe deeply. I started sobbing—deep retching sobs—until my body ached. I didn't know why. She told me that my unconscious housed memories of traumatic events that occurred before, during, and after my birth, and the pain associated with the incidents remained in me at the cellular level. So when I cried or raged, I released this poison and, once free, could experience a new birth, new life. I don't remember much from my early years, but she said that it didn't matter because the process worked anyway and that I would probably recall the traumatic situations later."

"Did you?"

"No, but I felt better when the sessions were over and wondered what it was that I didn't remember. Can you help me recover memories?"

"No, I don't work that way. Many techniques, like those used in rebirthing, put people into altered states of consciousness. I consider it not only unnecessary for solving problems, but sometimes dangerous. You can get lost in that realm, rather like wandering around a desert without a map or water. But tell me how did you get involved with est and psychics?"

"Well, the depth of the pain surprised me. Where did it come from? I figured that whatever was locked in my unconscious must prevent me from living a fulfilled life, and I wanted it uncovered so I could rectify the situation. Since the source of the problem was beyond my awareness, I consulted psychics and eventually sought help through the EST seminars."

"How long did you participate in EST?"

"From 1983 to now, about nine years. I still attend seminars."

"Do you feel better?"

"No, but I've learned a lot. I can't give up hope." Her eyes filled with tears.

"Yes, that would be devastating. What else are you doing?"

"This weekend some friends and I gathered in Boulder for a moon ceremony. We presented our dreams and requests to the moon."

I involuntarily winced and asked, "The moon? Why not talk to God?"

Amy's hair eclipsed her profile as she contemplated my suggestion, but suddenly she turned her head to stare intently at me. Her countenance had changed. Her vision cleared, as when someone cleanses a clouded lens, and she murmured, "I don't know. I could try."

"Yes, you could. Do try."

A month later as we were closing our session, Amy said, "While meditating at a Unity church last Sunday . . . well . . . um . . . an evil presence appeared in my mind. It was as real as you and me. Scared me to death! I stopped meditating, grabbed my things, and left. I've meditated for years, and that has never happened. Do you meditate?"

"Yes, I do, but I meditate or contemplate passages in the Bible. I don't release my will as you're encouraged to do in your practice. May I counsel you from a Christian perspective?"

"Yes, I'd like that."

"Then I'd like to pray with you." Amy smiled shyly, and I took her hands in mine. We bowed our heads, and I prayed, "Our Father, who art in heaven, hallowed be your name. Let your kingdom come in Amy's life. Your will be done on earth as it is in heaven. Give her daily bread, Lord, and forgive her sins, as she forgives those who sin against her. Lead her not into temptation and deliver her from evil. For thine is the kingdom and power and glory for ever and ever. Amen."

Amy withdrew her hand to wipe the tears from her cheeks and whispered, "Thank you, Sharon." Regaining her composure, she glanced at the small pamphlets from the Billy Graham ministry on the table next to her chair. "I'd like to read this. May I take it with me?"

"Yes, of course. And I'll see you next week."

At the close of each session in the following months, we prayed together, and then one day Amy arrived with the pamphlet in her hand. "Well, I did it!" she beamed. "I got down on my knees and accepted Jesus Christ as my Lord and Savior. I signed on the dotted line. I'm a Christian!"

I hugged her and said, "That's wonderful. Welcome to the kingdom! How did that happen?"

"Well, really I felt desperate, and it seemed like the only sane decision I could make," she grinned.

"Are you attending a church?" She nodded, and I asked, "Have you ever before?"

"Yes, when I was a teenager, I belonged to a church, but I couldn't stand the hypocrisy! I left."

"Yes, I understand. It's hard when people fail us, and when it happens in church it is tempting to assume that because people fall short, God is not who he says he is. That's why I left the church as a teen. But later I came back—just like the prodigal son. Do you remember that story in the Bible?"

"Yes, I do. I'm the prodigal."

"Well, so was I," I laughed. "And if your homecoming is anything like mine, you'll struggle for a while. You know Jesus came to save us not only from ourselves, but from Satan as well, God's enemy and ours. Satan doesn't let go easily, but he does as we love and obey Christ," I reassured her. "Becoming Christlike doesn't happen instantly. God takes us through many valleys and to the tops of mountains as he changes us. But the work is his, and we're to love and obey him."

Amy's eyes watered. "Well, that's a relief. I've worked hard on my own. I'm tired."

"Take heart," I said, touching her arm. "You've come home to the loving arms of God the Father! No other spiritual practice or religion can replicate the love and power of his Holy Spirit, who now resides within you. Oh, others have the words and philosophies, but none can transform you—that power belongs to God alone. It's really something to behold. People will disappoint you; that's a given." I added, "We get lots of practice forgiving one another."

"What should I do with my astrology books and other mementos? My friends would love them!"

"But why give them something you know doesn't work and destroys lives? Simply put them in the trash or fire." She smiled, and I added, "When I became a Christian, I converted my morning meditations to time spent reading the Bible and praying. I find it very helpful."

Later I suggested that Amy meet with Carrie, the woman who prayed with me when I first became a Christian. Carrie had read Neil Anderson's books, so I sent her a copy of *The Steps to Freedom in Christ* to use when she prayed with Amy.[7]

Amy described her conversion in this way: "When I accepted Jesus Christ as Lord and Savior, I felt no different and kept waiting for my burning bush experience, like Moses had. I actually felt the presence of God most when you and I prayed together. I put off calling Carrie until I was six days flat on my back with pneumonia. Then I called her, figured I'd have nothing to lose.

"Carrie and I prayed through the steps to freedom in Christ. I repented and renounced all my involvements, forgave anyone who ever hurt me, including myself, and affirmed my position in Christ. Immediately I felt peaceful and I knew my search was over. Finished. Nothing dramatic—just simple peace and a sense of completion. And then at church when the pastor asked, 'Who loves children?' my heart leaped, and I thought, 'I do.' So I volunteered to help in the primary grades, and it has been wonderful. I just want to give back, you know?"

---

7    Neil Anderson, *The Steps to Freedom in Christ* (Ventura, Calif.: Regal Books, 1995).

I nodded, "Yes, I know."

"Recently while attending a friend's church, I went forward for an altar call and acknowledged publicly that Jesus Christ is my Lord and Savior." She smiled sweetly, "I'm home. No more searching."

I smiled. I was happy for her.

I thought of other clients who had accepted Jesus Christ as Lord and Savior since my conversion and the remarkable transformation that occurred in their lives and mine. Yet I remained mindful of the many still deceived and separated from God. Whenever I'm asked I present my testimony, and through the process, I develop better ways of communicating what God has done for me.

In the winter of 1993 Dr. Gordon Lewis, a professor at Denver Seminary, invited me to present my testimony to twelve students enrolled in his class, Christianity and the Occult. I wound through the corridors, entered the classroom, and walked down the narrow aisle toward the podium. On either side, men and women warmly greeted me.

Seated before me were missionaries serving in Lithuania and Yugoslavia; two pastors—one a Baptist and the other a Chinese immigrant ministering to a small congregation in the Denver area—and students working toward Master of Divinity and counseling degrees.

Based on previous responses to my testimony, here and elsewhere, I anticipated that in spite of their faith in Jesus Christ, commitment to serve, and wealth of experience, some privately questioned if Satan and his army of demons actually wreaked the havoc described in the Bible. Perhaps the devil was more mythical than real, a metaphor for human failings or a pawn to divert personal responsibility for sin, as when someone coyly says, "The devil made me do it!"

But I knew there would be some who had confronted evil, heard troubling voices, sensed a malevolent presence, seen someone oppressed. I hoped that my testimony would strengthen their faith in the One who sets the captives free and would also encourage them to witness to the oppressed. "It's risky business to speak of diabolical entities with capabilities to commingle and control emotions, thoughts, and bodies," I began. "These beliefs seem more compatible with the Middle Ages than with our enlightened times. Researchers inevitably study what is measurable, and the supernatural does not lend itself to the scientific method. The physical and social sciences give sophisticated explanations for phenomena once attributed to the supernatural. Belief in demons, that is, spiritual beings with ability to invade the spirit, body, and soul of a person, seem archaic and more in the realm of superstition than what we consider real.

"The media, by contrast, portrays men, women, and children inhabited by, and at the mercy of malevolent spiritual forces. They're thrown against walls, tossed out windows. They foam at the mouth, act despicably . . . "

Members of the class listened intently, some nodding as I talked, "My rejection of God and denial of evil left me vulnerable to a lie of Satan, namely, that my mind, emotions, and body were my personal domain, and nothing of a spiritual nature could influence me without my permission. I denied the sovereignty of God and was ignorant of his enemy, Satan—his character, capabilities, and designs on my life. Let me tell you my story."

When I finished, the members of the class applauded, and a man raised his hand and asked, "Do the demons continue to bother you, and, if so, how do you handle it?"

"Yes, as the Bible says, Satan attacks me at opportune times, but no more or less than other Christians who are serious about their faith. I'm probably more in tune with the nuances of spiritual warfare, and I habitually repeat passages of Scripture and pray. As a new Christian, I expected God to stop the spiritual attacks immediately, to make it impossible for demons to harass me. When it continued, I was confused, but I eventually learned that God wanted me to put my faith in him, and as I did, he freed me."

The man continued with his questioning: "Would you say more about this, like how you manage yourself and, as we say, discern what is of God?"

"Early on I learned to keep my eyes fixed on Jesus and never to address demons or angels. I ignored them and talked only to God. Since demons can manipulate feelings, thoughts, and physical sensations, I learned to give my experience no ultimate authority. Sometimes people misinterpret this statement to mean I don't care about myself or never experience life fully, which of course is not true, because I do. What I am saying is that I've learned that I'm much more than what happens within my physical body. "I'm conditioned to step back from my experience.

"When describing how I survived when controlled by demons, I say that I retreated to a spiritual shelf, meaning that I learned to detach from my experience. I still step back to assess an experience and then direct myself accordingly. "Early in my conversion, I clung to Scripture and the Holy Spirit and trusted little else within me. Even after God restored me and I had a sense of self again, I was acutely aware of how my feelings, thoughts, and desires could throw me off course. Eventually I learned that the way I clung to God when I first knew him was where he wanted me to be. But as I got stronger, I found that my natural inclination was to rely on myself. It's a constant battle.

"So when making decisions, I wait for my initial responses to clear before acting. I pray, read Scripture, talk with others, and worship, and assume that God is in the midst of everything. When I ask, he always lets me know what to do; and when he does, I feel such peace, even though sometimes what he asks seems difficult."

Another hand went up. "When most oppressed, could you exercise your will?"

"Yes, even in the worst of it I could veto an impulse by simply not acting. Fortunately, I knew I was controlled by spirits and resisted incorporating their infusions into my behavior. I remembered who I once was and governed my behavior accordingly."

"What part did these involvements play in the breakup of your marriage?"

"The longer I meditated and delved into psychic phenomena, the more distant I felt from my husband, though the change was subtle and insidious. He instinctively mistrusted what I was doing, and when he challenged it, I treated his objections as personal attacks and distanced myself further. Eventually I saw him as an impediment to my spiritual growth and left. I remember thinking at the time that the universe would supply the people I needed if I remained true to my spiritual journey. That happened a couple of years before the spirits took control."

A woman to my right raised her hand and said, "My husband and I minister to gypsies, and I'd like to explain why the pastor asked the gypsies to leave the church when you were a teenager. Gypsies believe that baptism protects infants from evil spirits, and they approach many congregations to request baptism for their children. Babies receive numerous baptisms, and gypsies often hide jewelry or objects in the clothing of the child, believing that, once blessed, they become good-luck charms. They have no genuine interest in knowing God, and your minister was right in preventing them from disrupting your Sunday service."

"Thank you. Now, of course, I would simply ask him, but then I mistrusted all authority and looked for evidence to justify my rejection of the church and God." I shook my head. "I was very willful!"

A woman in the back of the room spoke. "I'm a missionary in Lithuania, and what you describe would have stunned me before entering the mission field, but since being overseas, I'm more aware of the demonic influences. Many foreign cultures encourage participation in occult rituals."

"Yes, and as our culture grows more accepting, I'm sure we'll see an increase of evidence here too. In fact, aren't we already?"

"Could you offer some advice about how to tell someone about Jesus Christ?"

"Yes, although I suspect you have more to teach me than I you. First, pray. Pray for the person deceived as well as for guidance for yourself. Second, share the love of Christ. Nothing in New Age thinking or the occult replicates the love of Christ, and underneath the sophisticated words and philosophies lies an empty heart and a vacant, cold, restless spirit. Remember that the battle is for the heart and mind. Third, present the gospel, but try not to be argumentative. Sprinkle your conversation with Scripture. Fourth, if someone relates a supernatural experience, try not to minimize or discredit it; rather, tell that person that you also believe in an unseen universe but that not every spirit is from God. Teach what you know to be true. Lastly. remember that God prepares hearts to hear the gospel. One plants a seed and another reaps. We don't know how

God will use us, but he does command us to preach the good news."

Before I gave such talks, I prayed that God would prepare the hearts and minds of those attending. I asked that his Spirit strengthen the faith of believers and mercifully ready the hearts of unbelievers to hear the good news. I prayed that he would thwart the Enemy's attempts to interfere during our time together.

Occasionally people in the audience offered that the circumstances of my life dismayed them. Nothing like that had happened to them, and they failed to see the relevancy to their lives. A greater number talked about friends, family members, or neighbors who participated in occult activities or explored a counterfeit religion. I heard repeatedly, "My, I wish they were here."

I closed these sessions by saying, "God saved us from the work of Satan and ourselves, and though I think it important to understand how Satan attempts to destroy our faith in God, the Bible tells us to keep our attention on Jesus Christ and his Word. As we love and obey him, his righteousness shines in us and he delivers us from harm's way."

When I was finished I offered to pray with people, and some came forward. It was then that I heard such statements as these:

"I visited a psychic three years ago, and my life hasn't been the same."

"I'm awakened in the middle of the night. I get scared."

"Sometimes I hear voices—I know it's not my thoughts.

"I see a spirit figure in my bedroom at night. It frightens me."

"I was involved like you. Would you help me become a Christian? Would you pray with me?"

I assured them that God sent his Son, Jesus Christ, to save us from the works of Satan. I said, "Jesus wants us to draw close to him when we are afraid or attacked by the Adversary. During these times, call on Jesus Christ. He's waiting to hear from you."

Then we prayed, cried, and laughed, and together we drew closer to God.

# CHAPTER 19

# Send Me, Lord!

*Then I heard the voice of the Lord saying, "Whom shall I send?
And who will go for us?"*

*And I said, "Here am I. Send me!"* (Isa. 6:8).

**Fall 1994**

THE MORNING SUN SHIMMERED OFF the glass top of the
dining room table, twinkling at me across the room as I settled
into a well-stuffed chair and retrieved my Bible from the floor.
Slender leaves drooped on a five-foot houseplant above the table.
I curled my feet under me and opened to Ephesians, sipped hot
coffee, and mentally prepared to talk with God—to read, write,
and pray.

I opened the Bible to Ephesians, and midway through, my
sleepy stupor receded, and I read, "Although I am less than the
least of all the Lord's people, this grace was given me" (Eph. 3:8).

Imagine Paul, the great evangelist, calling himself the least of
all God's people, and yet I understood. As my relationship with
God deepened, I became more aware of his holiness as well as my
sin and natural proclivity to rely on myself and not love others as
I should. I pictured Paul sitting in prison alone with God. Paul

was humbled by his abject reliance on the grace of God, and all I could say was, "Me too."

I flipped pages back to the Old Testament and stopped at the book of Jonah. I smiled, remembering how as a child I shuddered when hearing about Jonah in the belly of the whale. "How did he breathe?" I would ask, never daring to ponder the slime and stench in the great stomach.

I now read in Jonah, "The word of the LORD came to Jonah son of Amittai: 'Go the great city of Nineveh and preach against it, because its wickedness has come up before me.' But Jonah ran away from the LORD . . . " (1:1–3). I mused at Jonah's foolishness and said, "Jonah, where could you hide from God?" I continued reading about how a storm terrified the men onboard the ship, and they awakened Jonah to see if an action of his had caused the turbulence. He replied, "I am a Hebrew and I worship the LORD, the God of heaven, who made the sea and the land. . . . Throw me into the sea, . . . I know that it is my fault" (vv. 9, 12). They finally believed Jonah and threw him in.

Jonah's obstinacy never dissuaded God from his purposes. God was God, and his will would be done! Jonah would have to change, and evidently God thought this was best accomplished inside a fish. "Jonah, you and I are stubborn people. You ended up sitting in stench, and I ended up infested with demons. God will be heard!"

I read on: "In my distress I called to the LORD, and he answered me. From deep in the realm of the dead I called for help, and you listened to my cry. You hurled me into the depths, . . . the deep surrounded me" (2:2, 5).

Sobered, I found that passages from Hebrews came to mind: "It is a dreadful thing to fall into the hands of the living God" (10:31). And later in the book: "God is a consuming fire" (12:29).

I prayed, "Lord, you forced me to glimpse hell, where some will spend eternity, and yet how soon I forget. How tempting it is to deny the reality of it when I'm secure in my living room; Lord, have mercy on me."

I read on in Jonah, "But you, LORD my God, brought my life up from the pit. . . . Those who cling to worthless idols turn away from God's love for them. . . . Salvation comes from the LORD" (2:6b, 8, 9b).

Sensing the Lord's correction, as when he is about to reveal a sin, I stilled. My eyes riveted to the final passage of Jonah, "And should I not have concern for the great city of Nineveh, in which there are more than a hundred and twenty thousand people who cannot tell their right hand from their left—and also many animals?" (4:11).

Still blinded to my sin, I asked, "What does this have to do with me, Lord?" During the last two years, the plight of the deceived had seemed less relevant than maintaining my private practice, settling into a new marriage and home, and helping my son transition from high school to college. Had I run from God? No.

But God looked at the condition of my heart and did not like what he saw. He noted that while I was busy securing my life, I had lost my passion for pleasing him. Pride and concern for my reputation had replaced the enthusiasm I once had when praying to and serving him. Whereas before I had frequently told others about Christ's victory over darkness, in recent years I had sometimes encountered dismay, disapproval, or disbelief from Christians and had instinctively protected myself by sharing less and less.

I cried, "Oh, my God, forgive my pride and disobedience." Overwhelmed by his conviction, I pleaded, "Lord, forgive my fear, my turning from you. You are my only hope, and without you I am lost. Let me serve you, Lord."

Weeping and resting my head in my hands, I whispered, "They don't know their right hand from their left, just like me, Lord, just like me." Did I know in the days when I had to ask, "Am I hungry?" Or in the nights when I gazed at dancing shadows to divert my attention from the demonic drama in my mind? Did I know my right hand from my left as I pleaded for mercy from evil while demons mocked my groveling and heightened their attacks on my mind and body? Did I know years earlier when I put my faith in synchronized happenings and my intuition, in visions and moments of ecstasy that promised peace but delivered despair? Or when my hopes were dashed, did I know why, instead of receiving comfort, I was blamed for the demise? Or why I scrambled to right the wrong by relying more fervently on my thoughts to pull me through—go here; no, there; avoid this; no, that's not right; try again; it's up to me—until I was exhausted?

I knew not my right hand from my left or that Jesus Christ shed his blood and rose from the dead to save me that through his church "the manifold wisdom of God should be made known to the rulers and authorities in the heavenly realm" (Eph. 3:10). "Satan is a defeated foe, but many blindly walk to his eternal torment," I whispered. "How easy it is to forget the war and that the battle is for souls and that you, God, look to us, your church, to make your Way known. Yes, Lord, I forget."

I raised my head, put my Bible on the floor next to the chair, leaned forward, and clasped my hands in front of me. "Who will believe me? How will I find the words?" Then I thought, "When he calls, God provides the ways and means, and if I don't write this testimony, he will put me in the belly of a whale."

I smiled. The sternness of God's rebuke convinced me that if I refused him, none of my endeavors would succeed, and instead of being a vessel for the fruit of his Spirit, I would shrivel up and be empty, unfulfilled. I complied because I loved him. My marching orders clear, I prayed aloud, "Thank you, Lord. More than anything I want to please you. Send me."

# Epilogue

THROUGHOUT THE YEARS SINCE I first shared my story, many people have asked me for help when they have seen or sensed a demonic presence or are unsure of the source of supernatural phenomena. I discovered that most Christians need basic biblical teaching on what demons can and cannot do; instruction on how to test the spirits; and most important, confidence and increased faith in the power and authority of Jesus Christ over the demonic realm.

Christian Discernment Resources offers biblical teaching and support to think about such things, as well as guidance for testing the source of supernatural experiences, practices, and writings. Look for future books in bookstores, Amazon, and Kindle on the following subjects.

- Angels, demons, and the dead

- Spiritual oppression, demonization, deliverance, and mental illness

- Visions, intuitions, dreams, and meditation

- Eastern meditation, yoga, and energy therapies.

*But solid food is for the mature, who by constant use have trained themselves to distinguish good from evil* (Heb. 5:14).

# An Excerpt from
## *Angels, Demons, and the Dead*
### *by Sharon Beekmann*

FOURTEEN-YEAR-OLD STACY INHERITED a roommate and new sister when her mother remarried. Stacy had never met anyone like Dee, who had lived on the streets since age fifteen and developed a nasty drug habit. During the transition, Dee joined her dad's new family to "get clean." Stacy made it her mission to help her.

"Sister, I'm here!" nineteen-year-old Dee announced as she flung her backpack on the spare bed. Stacy gave Dee clothes, and they talked nonstop until eleven each night. After their talks, Dee routinely climbed out the bedroom window and joined her friends on the streets, returning the next morning while Stacy was at school. But one night the unthinkable happened—Dee died on a downtown sidewalk from an overdose. Guilt burdened Stacy's tender heart. "If only I had listened better and said more. She might have made it."

Four months later, out of the corner of her eye Stacy saw a phantom-like figure dash into her closet. She turned to face it, but nothing was there. She quivered as a slight chill came over her. She shrugged it off and went to bed. The next week, Stacy opened her eyes around midnight and calmly stared at an ill-formed spirit in her closet. "Is that Dee?" Shaking her head, she thought, "No. I'm dreaming." She drifted back to sleep. A couple nights later,

Stacy awoke and stared into the eyes of the spirit Dee. "What are you doing here?" Stacy blurted out as she sat up.

"I need to talk," the spirit girl said, "I didn't want to die. I'm so sorry. I don't want to be here. I wish I had listened to you. Help me." They communicated through their thoughts, though occasionally Stacy spoke out loud. After a half hour, the spirit Dee unexpectedly vanished. Stacy wondered where she went and if she would return.

She did return, and for the next six months, she and Stacy talked several times a week. Dee always began with, "I need to talk," and then repeated verbatim what she had said the first time she appeared. One day Stacy saw Dee's spirit standing beside her friends at school. As Stacy chatted with friends, Dee spoke into Stacy's mind in a demanding tone, "I need to talk!" From that day on, Dee dominated and bullied Stacy and followed her everywhere saying, "It's your fault that I died. Pay attention to me. I don't like it here!"

Finally, Stacy confided in her mother, who was a Christian. She told Stacy to stop talking to Dee and to immediately recite the Lord's prayer whenever the spirit appeared. Then they prayed together. Others prayed with and for Stacy, and she learned what the Bible had to say about the dead. The spirit stopped appearing.

Stacy's story, inspired by actual events, resembles those told by Christians and nonbelievers who have seen or sensed the presence of the dead. The encounters, whether once or ongoing, are emotionally charged and intensely personal. Generally, they are private matters, rarely discussed with others. But years later people can recall where they were, what was said, and how they felt.

Christians often ask the following questions.

1. Can the dead communicate with the living? If so, why do some people see them and others not?

2. How is a person to know if they are speaking to the dead or a demon? Given that Christians have the Holy Spirit, shouldn't they be able to sense the difference?

3. Some report getting into trouble like Stacy, but many say there are comforted by their talks with a deceased husband or wife. What is the harm?

The Bible answers these and other questions. It doesn't say a lot about the dead, but it tells us enough. . . .

CPSIA information can be obtained
at www.ICGtesting.com
Printed in the USA
LVHW04s1102220918
591006LV00001B/43/P